To David

The Boston Globe

KEYS FINAL

Miami

TUESDAY, SEPTEMBER 21

Whale migration reaches S.

Key West, FL

Maritime Michelangelo
Artist unafraid of big statements takes love of seas to Be

SHOW
ENTERTAINMENT NEWS, REVIEWS AND PERSONALITIES

Whaling Wa

USA
TODAY

NO. 1 IN THE USA . . . FIRS

Crowd gathers for whaling party

After long wet wait, whale artist paints

Wall gets weary artist's finishing touches
Wyland scurried to complete it for today's dedication.

Artist expresses love of sea, on a large scale

wy

AND

Whale

Tales from America's

Leading Marine Life Artist

Whale Tales

Copyright © 1995 Wyland Studios

Artwork © 1995 Wyland

All rights reserved

First published in U.S.A. by Wyland Studios
2171 Laguna Canyon Road, Laguna Beach, CA U.S.A. 92651

Library of Congress Catalog Card Number 94-60366

ISBN-0-9631793-5-7

Cover - Original Oil by Jim Warren and Wyland ©1993
Manufactured in United States of America

Produced by:
Wyland Studios
2171 Laguna Canyon Road, Laguna Beach, CA U.S.A. 92651

Dedication

Whale Tales is dedicated to my family, who have stood by me through thick and thin. Mom, who is now Vice President of Wyland Studios has been a point of light guiding my life and career. My three brothers were always there for me. Steve, owner of Wyland Galleries in Portland, Oregon, once beat me in an art contest and now enjoys selling my art. He's awesome. Bill and I have become very close in the past few years. He is president of Wyland Galleries, Hawaii, and a guy with a great vision. Tom is my youngest brother and was always there to help me in any way. Tom and his wife, Valerie were vital to the success of the East Coast Tour. And my dad, Robert Wyland, who will always be the best dad in the world.

I love you guys.

Special Thanks

First, I would like to thank Angela Eaton, who is not only beautiful, but super talented, helping me see the book through its genesis. Mark Doyle wrote my first book with me, and we continue our collaboration in *Whale Tales*. He's a great writer, listener and friend. Jennifer Mueller is my art director, designer and creative genius. Sylvia Bass is my personal assistant and quite an artist herself. Hilary Merritt is my accountant and one superwoman. Sondra Augenstein is my special events coordinator, who I think is the greatest dynamo ever. Dick Lyday, and Everbest Printing, Booklines Hawaii, The Venema Group, Natural Wonders, Peter Paul, Don Dixon, Mark and Debbie Ferrari, Tom Klingenmeier, my collectors, friends old and new, the thousands of volunteers who have contributed their heart and soul to the Whaling Wall project, the Wyland Studios crew, Wyland Galleries and all of Team Wyland!

CONTENTS

... There is no rest when you're on planetary duty...

-Wyland

Introduction

*T*elling tales has always been easy for me. Ever since I was very young, I enjoyed both hearing and telling a good story. Lucky for me, my life has provided me with many experiences that sometimes are almost impossible to believe. Some stories border on the humorous, sad, ridiculous, amazing, crazy and absurd — all part of this lifestyle known simply as "artist."

Someone once told me that in France I would be an artiste, but in the United States I would be just another painter. Try to go to the bank and get a loan as an artist. . . right.

Never in my wildest dreams did I ever think I would one day receive international acclaim for something that seemed so easy and natural. Artists were never appreciated until long after they were dead. But I'm alive, and still young by artist years. Yeah, I had my share of critics and naysayers. But overall, my art was receiving accolades, not only in the United States, but around the world.

Believe me, I'm probably the most surprised of all. Right place, right time? Hardly. When I started painting whales and dolphins in 1971, the environmental movement had barely begun. I couldn't give my paintings away. But, as

1

consciousness grew, so did appreciation for my art. It was always my hope that, in some small way, my art could make a difference. *People* magazine asked a writer friend of mine, "How could painting a whale on a wall save a whale?" I still believe it may very well be the only thing that can.

Not everyone is going to be able to see whales eye to eye like I have. But if they can see them depicted in these giant murals, I feel they will want to get involved in protecting them.

Why whales? One only needs to see a whale to answer that. I truly believe when we see whales we become changed humans. After I first saw gray whales migrating along the California coast, I knew I was different. My spirit was lifted, and I haven't touched the ground yet. People ask if I will ever paint anything else. Yes and no. To me, the whale is one of God's greatest creatures and a symbol of the environment. There could be no greater creature to lead us down the path of consciousness and not convenience.

When I was a kid, like kids today, I admired the dinosaurs. Later, I realized they still live in our oceans. The dinosaurs were gone, but what about the great whales? How could we help them? I was inspired by watching Jacques Cousteau on television in the early '70s. What could

Introduction

I possibly do?

After years of filling canvas after canvas with my favorite subjects, I decided I needed larger canvasses. So I started looking at the sides of buildings. When I completed the first Whaling Wall, I decided I would paint 100 walls throughout the world. Along the way, I embarked on a journey that has kept me in motion for over 20 years. There's no rest when you're on planetary duty.

This book has brought back many memories of what I call "the good old bad old good old days." The classic starving artist born in Detroit by mistake. The ugly politics of painting the first Whaling Walls, meeting the friendly gray whales and swimming eye to eye with the humpback whales.

At one point, I was dragged into court for giving a Whaling Wall to Honolulu. And how unusual I must have looked painting whales in the heart of Japan's whaling cities. I think this was the first time many Japanese had seen whales other than on their dinner plates.

Probably my favorite story is when my brother Bill and I were reunited as roommates down under — The Odd Couple, Part II. Then I took on the system by painting a wall at 3 a.m. under the cover of darkness. To quote the great

Whale Tales

Bart Simpson: "Eat my shorts, man." And I'll never forget the craziness of painting the largest mural in the world in only six weeks. We had a riot in L.A.

So dive in. . . the water's fine.

Best Fishes,

WYLAND

1

Starving Artist

...The first artist was God. He's still the best...

·ᴡᵧᴸᴀᴺᴼ

*W*aking up at 4 a.m. in icy Detroit is an experience even the crustiest of Marine sergeants might have a hard time forgetting. In the dead of winter, Detroit, in and of itself, is bad enough. But to be jolted out of a warm slumber to face this wintery haven before daylight? No way. . . leave me alone. . . this is not funny. . . I'm sleeping. . . this must be a nightmare. . . go away.

Ohh, but it *was* happening. My mom was shaking me violently so I could get up and get ready for my first job. At age 16, the last time I'd seen 4 a.m. I was making my way out of this woman's womb. It was a rude awakening then, and it was a rude awakening now. Could it be possible that other people got out of bed at this ungodly hour just so they could wash their faces, get dressed and then stumble out of their warm cozy homes to go to work?

Well, my mother sure thought so. I didn't exactly grow up with a silver spoon in my mouth. My dad left us when I was four, and my mom worked long hours at the Chrysler factory to put food on the table for me and my three brothers. By then, it was 1972 and I was already an artist and painting constantly, working very hard at it. But these were tough times, and my mom felt it was time to expose me to what the real world was all about — a job.

Only problem was, I didn't really have a job, not yet anyway. I was up, sort of, freshly showered, wearing my very best clothes and apprehensive as hell about what the day held in store for me. Yes, I was determined to honor my mother's wishes and experience those proverbial rights of passage into early manhood. But why did it have to be this early?

Instead of being over the hill and through the woods, the closest Day Workers' office was over the tracks and through some of the worst slums Detroit had to offer. It was bitter cold, and the sky was dark gray as my mom gently slid our old car up to a chewed up curb in front of a crummy old building distinguished only by the long line of people bundled up against the cruel chill outside the front door. My initial observation was that this was a mob of transients, bums and unfortunate people out of work. And that's exactly what it was. Detroit, then the murder capital of the world, a bombed out city still in shock over years of race riots and mounting unemployment, had been particularly hard on this lot. And it was my great honor to have the opportunity to hop out of our warm car and join the end of this dreary procession. I can't be sure, but I like to think my mother felt some strong apprehension of her own as she pulled away from the curb. She had just pushed one of her offspring out into the open water to swim on his own. Instead of a beautiful stream or river, though, this water looked more like a frozen cesspool.

Well, I could fill several chapters describing this depressing scene, but I don't want to appear like I'm whining about my humble beginnings. Basically, the drill was this: you stood in line for several hours before you got inside the door, where the line would inch up to a desk, where you registered and then sat down and waited for them to call your name. If you were given a job, you were then loaded into a truck and carted off to the worst factory jobs in the city.

Whale Tales

From what I can remember, we were paid about two bucks an hour, and you had to give the Day Workers' office one. I'm not certain this was correct, but this is my memory — it was something ugly.

What surprised me most was that I wasn't even chosen for one of these coveted positions on the first day, or on the second day for that matter. Now, I had always been told that if you were going to go get a job, you had to get cleaned up and shave and dress nice, which I did. Every morning for three days, we drove down at 5 a.m., and I sat there for a good six hours without having my named called. As I left the office for the second day in a row, an old guy with a beard stopped me. I guess he spotted dejection on my well scrubbed face.

"Hey, I saw you here yesterday," his hoarse voice said in an attempted whisper. "You really look clean. You gotta look more like you need a job, man. Next time, don't shave; don't shower. You're never gonna get a job lookin' like that."

"But I was always told you have to get cleaned up and look good to get a job," I protested, no longer believing this April Fool's myth myself.

"Noooo, man, not here, not here," he said, shaking his shaggy head. "Look at these people. You gotta fit in, man. You gotta look like you NEED a job!"

Even though he himself was definitely dressed to look like he needed a job, I decided not to ask him why he was still waiting in the office for the second day in a row. That night, I slept in my clothes, and the next morning I didn't shower or shave. I tried to look as cruddy as I could, and damned if it didn't work. The next morning, the man at the desk looked me over and said, "You look like you need a job." I said, "Yessir," and he gave me one.

I guess I should have seen it coming. There's something wrong about having to dress down to get a job. There were a couple of broken-down buses waiting like limousines in the back of the building for us, but I recall filing into an open-ended truck, just like in The Great Depression. I mean, there was no dignity in this, no dignity whatsoever. I remember thinking at this moment that this was not what my mom had in mind for me.

It didn't matter. My thoughts quickly turned, along with those of the 40 or so other poor souls in the back of the truck, to the freezing weather outside. Besides being dubbed the

"Motor City," Detroit is famous for its arctic winters. It was literally snowing and raining ice at the same time. We were freezing to death as this rickety old truck rambled down an endless maze of greasy, pothole-filled factory streets.

I'll never forget finally being let out of the back of the vehicle. I was clearly the youngest one, with most of the men around the age of 50. As we neared the noisy area of the factory, we were told by an ugly man with a booming Midwestern voice that we were going to be working a 12-hour shift, and that we were to do precisely as we were told. Then the man who would be our foreman came over to me and said, "I need you to run this machine, ever done it?"

"Of course," I said, lying. I was pretty smart and felt I could do anything.

"Alright, listen," he yelled above the noise of the machinery. "I want you to run this steel machine, okay?"

No problem. All I had to do was step on a pedal, push a button, step on the pedal, push a button — for 12 hours. After two hours of this, my mind started to wander big time, and I thought to myself, "Any idiot or monkey could do this." I started to think about my artwork and some of the things I could have been doing with it, when all of a sudden

I pushed the button twice instead of pushing the pedal. The machine broke down within seconds. From out of nowhere the foreman materialized looking very upset and calling me every name in the book. He was a huge, greasy, hairy monster of a man, at least 280 pounds. Needless to say, I was quite intimidated. As the brute worked feverishly to fix the machine, he ran out of names to call me and started at the top of his list calling me the same names again. I guess repetition is a way of life in the factories.

He finally left and I got started again, pushing the pedal, then the button and so on. Almost immediately I'm thinking, "Jeez, I've got a brain. I'm an intelligent person. I'm an artist, and this is just not taking advantage of. . . BAM!" Within minutes I had pushed the pedal twice and debilitated the machine once more. This time, the foreman came over rather slowly, shaking his head. I was no longer even worthy of any more names. Besides, it's always been my experience that the feeble-minded usually exhaust their ability to insult someone once they've exhausted their repertoire of profanity. He just fixed the piece of equipment and walked off, his head moving from side to side in disgust.

Well, I was so intelligent that I broke the machine down a

third time! The foreman, who, but a few hours earlier, had been my industrial mentor, came rushing over from across the room screaming, "Get your little ass out of here right now! You're fired!"

Fired! I never expected this. Maybe I had to dress down to even get this stinking job, but I was just too smart to get fired! I walked out of the factory dazed and confused. The only thing I could think of was that I hadn't finished my 12-hour shift — I had only put in four or five hours. What was I going to tell my mom? Heartbroken and ashamed that I had been fired from my very first job, I started walking the long five miles back home. It was like I was on automatic pilot; my eyes never left the cold pavement as I walked. Suddenly, about half-way, I saw the neon sign of a doughnut shop reflecting off the icy sidewalk, and I sort of veered toward it and through the front door, instinctively knowing there was no way I could go home and admit I'd been fired. I stayed there in a back booth all day drinking coffee, formulating a credible story and basically doing my best to recover from the whole traumatic episode.

That evening when I arrived home, the first thing out of my mom's mouth was "How was work?" A gallon of caffeine had perfected my lie: "Great, mom, it was fine. I'm looking forward to going back tomorrow," I said, quickly moving on to my room. Fortunately, she didn't push for details.

Next morning, same procedure as the previous three days. Four a.m., groggy son piling into the car to go to his new job, another fine day in a vapid industrial American city. On the way, I didn't say anything when my mom asked why in the world I was wearing the same wrinkled, dirty clothes I had worn the day before. It was too early in the morning to find a smooth way of telling her I was dressing for success.

The line outside the Day Workers' office was exceptionally long this day, but I endured it without complaint because I was determined to redeem myself if I got another chance at a job. When I finally made my way up to the registration desk, the man calling out names gave me one of those knowing "I've got the goods on you" looks. But to my surprise, he was rather civil and actually said, "Heard you got fired yesterday."

"That's right," I said meekly.

"Well, that sometimes happens the first time," he said,

looking down at the clipboard in his hand. "We have another job for you if you want to work."

"Yessir!" I shot back.

"Alright, get out to the truck."

The truck, though just as cold and rattletrap as it'd been the day before, didn't bother me this time. I was on a mission. I would show them. Yesterday had just been a bizarre mishap. No more daydreaming. No more shithead foreman. No more coffee marathons. No more lying at home. I couldn't wait to get there.

Little did I know that I almost would have been better off if I had jumped off the back of the truck as it lumbered along the busy streets and been run over and killed by a bus. Even to a young artist with a vivid imagination, this new factory, new only in that is was different from the last one, was the closest thing to hell I could ever envision.

There was fire; there was unbelievable noise; there were grinding pipes and steel that made your ears feel like they were breaking. It was louder than any rock music I had ever listened to. This was an iron works factory, earpiercing and smelly. You couldn't escape the smell, and your eyes watered constantly. It was the most unhealthy environment in which to spend even five minutes, much less 12 hours! It was no wonder they had a lot of turnover here. When workers refused to return for another day, those who stayed moved "up" in position. That left the new guys — like me — with the most physical, dangerous jobs. I mean, these were horrible, horrible jobs.

To top it all off, our foreman, who was a couple of hundred pounds lighter than the pig who had fired me the day before, looked as if he'd been born to carry a whip and serve as the demonic toilmaster of this foul worksite. He was greasy, ill-tempered and, instead of using a whip, possessed a megaphone voice with which he simultaneously lashed out instructions and insults to his bewildered charges.

The harsh instructions he bellowed out to me were to take a shovel and throw iron ore down into a steel barrel that lay at the bottom of an eight-foot pit. Still determined to perform and prove myself, I filled the barrel in about 45 minutes and was feeling pretty good about it. I felt, hey, I was accomplishing something and working up a sweat. The foreman also had instructed me that, when the barrel was full, I was to walk over and pull on two chains. One chain would make the barrel come up, and the other chain would make it move over and dump the load onto a conveyor belt. Because of the deafening noise, however, I somehow forgot which chain did what; they both looked alike. I went over and, after a moment's hesitation, pulled one of them. Instead of the barrel moving over to the conveyor belt, it simply raised a bit and dumped the entire load right back into the pit, with the barrel sitting upside down on top of the iron ore.

Of course I freaked out. I instantly thought to myself, "Oh my god, I screwed up again." I jumped down into the hole and started shovelling the ore laying all over the pit back into the barrel, working frantically to finish before anyone saw me. I was so panicky that I ignored the sharp ore that filled my shoes and socks, cutting my ankles and legs. A half-hour later I finished and climbed out and walked back to the chains. The noise, the stress, the adrenaline, I don't know — I was so disoriented that I still wasn't sure which chain to pull and, yes, yanked on the same one I had pulled earlier, dumping the same load right back into the pit again.

The whole thing was a nightmare. At this point, the nasty toilmaster came running up, pissed out of his mind.

"What in the hell do you think you're doing?" he yelled at me. "Get that bucket filled up and get it on the conveyor belt! You're holding up the whole factory!"

Once again I jumped down into the dagger-like ore, shovelled it into the barrel, climbed out of the pit, ran over to the chains and, believe it or not, pulled the same damn chain for a third time. As I was standing there stunned by my own disbelief, I felt this hard, steel-toed boot kick me right in the ass. I whirled around and found myself face-to-face with the weasel-faced foreman, who yelled at the top of his lungs, "GET THE HELL OUT OF HERE — YOU'RE FIRED!"

Now I had heard the day before from one of the guys that if you get fired three times from the Day Workers' office, it looks real bad on your record. In fact, he said, "For your whole life this will be on your record. You'll never get another job." I had lasted less than three hours in this factory from hell, my second career path in two days — cut short. I was feeling real depressed, two strikes against me, one more and I'd be blackballed from industrial America forever.

That afternoon I got to know the waitress at the doughnut shop very well. A kind, maternal soul, she listened to my entire life story. You know, how I was really an artist and didn't really want to do this anyway, and how horrible the factories were and how they had treated me so terribly. I had no money, but she poured me free coffee for nine hours. Daunted but not defeated, I told my real mom that night that the job wasn't bad and that I'd be going back the next day. I laid awake all night thinking about how I only had one more chance, and that if I blew it a third time I might never work again.

It's not hard to understand the pathos of a 16-year-old who had never had any career counseling. This dreadful factory work had somehow come to symbolize the rest of working world for me, and I didn't like it at all. But one thing that has always stayed with me, sometimes to my own disadvantage, is a spirit of never giving up. The Day Worker guy looked at me quizzically as I approached his desk the next morning. "Twice," he said straight off. "Twice, you were fired twice. You know, if you get fired three times . . ."

"I know, I know!" I said, loud enough for everyone in the room to hear.

"You want to go back out," he asked.

"Yeah, I definitely do," I said, wondering why I said the

word "definitely."

I'll never forget this last job. Another grimy factory, another chance to complete a 12-hour shift. This time I was working with two other guys, much older than I was, and our job was to take pipes of three different sizes and put them into these boxes that had little holes in the tops of them. You took a pipe and put it in the hole, took another pipe and put it in the hole. I don't know what these two men wanted to do with the rest of their lives but, after two hours of putting pipes in holes, all three of us stopped for a few minutes, looked at each other, and said almost in unison: "What the hell are we doing this for? Let's get out of here."

As for me, I was so depressed I just wanted to drown my sorrows a little and forget about this whole employment experience. So the three of us slipped out to a liquor store and bought a bottle of Jack Daniels. It was what white collars might call a long lunch. We all knew we were throwing in the towel on this job. We were going to go back, but if we got fired, so what? After drinking the Jack, we went back to the boxes with the holes in much better spirits. We started to make a game of throwing the pipes into the boxes, using basketball tosses. We were backing up, shooting from the perimeter, just acting crazy. After a little of that, I decided to draw pictures on the boxes. The holes on top became certain parts of the female anatomy, and it became our new sport to score in a different way. Before long, the foreman, whom I was too intoxicated to even remember, walked up and saw what we were doing. He looked over the drawings I had made on the boxes and asked all three of us to leave the premises at once.

I was doomed, doomed. It hit me harder than I thought it would before we drank the whiskey. I'd never be able to get another job, I thought. It was the lowest point in my life. I couldn't get any lower. But good things can often grow out of the gloomiest of disasters. I went home that night and literally locked myself into my room. My mom, sensing something was wrong, stood at the door and asked if I wanted to go to work the next day. "No," I told her with a powerful new conviction. "I'm an artist. I have to do my art." The whole thing had been a real awakening. I decided right then that I would work as hard as I could to become a professional artist and never go back to a hellhole factory again. For some reason my mom understood and said, "fine." She never asked me to look for a job again.

The next six months, I worked night and day in our basement on my drawing, on my painting, on my sculpture, on everything until I put together an incredible portfolio. One evening my mom came in and showed me an article that had appeared in *The Detroit News* about a famous airbrush artist named Shrunken Head. Considered by many to be one of the best airbrush artists in the world, his real name was Dennis Poosch. He lived in Detroit where he was doing quite well air-brushing fantastic murals on vans. I guess what caught my mother's eye in the article was that Shrunken Head had a great interest in Salvador Dali, who she knew was my favorite artist.

"Why don't you go down and see this guy and see if he'll hire you?" she asked.

At first I said no, but after thinking it over, I asked myself, "Why not?" I put together my portfolio, found his studio and went up and pounded on his door. Now this was no ordinary door; it was a psychedelic purple with a small head in the middle of it that looked like a wrinkled up apple. It looked like a shrunken head, but it was probably plastic. It had long black straggly hair and a bone through its nose.

Suddenly the purple door swung open, and there stood a larger living replica of the creepy little door ornament. It was him, Shrunken Head. Only, instead of being some kind of pagan cannibal, he was just a very friendly hippie, and very cool.

"Hi, Dennis," I said, very nervously. "I read your article in *The Detroit News*, and I'd like to show you my portfolio."

"Come on in and let's see what you got," he said, motioning me in.

The studio was huge. There were outrageous murals and canvasses everywhere. A set of stairs led down to a cavernous floor where at least 20 custom vans sat with their sides, backs and front-ends covered with brilliant murals in various stages of completion. This was a big, big operation; two Doberman Pinschers were loping around the joint, stopping every now and then to sniff me and let me know they ran the place.

We sat down and looked through my book, and after a few minutes Shrunken Head said, "So, you're into Dali?"

"Yeah," I replied.

"Me, too. This work is incredible. You're very talented. Have you ever done any airbrush?"

24

"Not really," I told him. "But I think I can do it."

He led me downstairs where he was half-way done with a van. He started painting, and I settled in behind him to watch. At one point, I was so close that my head was literally resting on his shoulder. He reached back without looking and gave me a little spray of paint in the face to back me off. He had to do this a couple of times, but neither of us minded, really. We were on the same wavelength.

"You think you can do this?" he asked, handing me the gun. Without answering, I took it and sat down. "Finish it," he said.

To my great amazement, he left and didn't come back for several hours. I mean, here was a $4,000 custom mural, and he just handed it to me. I could have destroyed the whole thing. It was like learning to swim; he just threw me into the water. I made a hundred mistakes, dripping paint all over the place. But, in each place I dripped, I transformed the mistake into a rock, which has since become sort of a trademark for me.

Dennis came back a few hours later and viewed my work. To make a long story short, he hired me on the spot, and I worked under his tutelage for four months. This is where I learned how to use all kinds of spray guns, including the larger ones for putting in background colors. We did all the big auto shows in Detroit, painting murals on the sides of vans, drawing large audiences to watch us work. This, I guess, is where I first started painting in public, an invaluable learning experience that has served me extremely well on my Whaling Wall project.

Working for Dennis Poosch was a groundbreaker for me. Shrunken Head Studios was my first job in my chosen profession, and I'll forever be in this man's debt. In addition to training me in all the tools of the trade, he showed me that I, too, could go out and do it. I could be a working artist, doing exactly what I loved to do. He was a great mentor for me, and I worked 12-hour shifts for him without even thinking about it. In fact, I often spent the night at the studio working all day and all night.

As I look back, I now realize that my short career in the Detroit factories was really a Godsend. I can be a very spiritual person, and I firmly believe I was sent to those jobs so I could learn how to appreciate the talent I had and develop it. Ironically, the experience taught me about work ethic. I bore down tirelessly on my artwork and haven't stopped since. I still work very hard every day because I never want to go back to that dark world. I still have the fear. It's very real for me, and it's very real for a lot of people. I was lucky. I'll never have to push the button and step on the pedal again.

2

The Politics of Painting the First Wall

*...In France I would be an 'artiste,' but in America
I'm just another painter...*

WYLAND

One day in 1971, Mom decided she was going to take her
four boys to California to visit her sister, my Aunt Linda, who
lived in the Los Angeles area. She loaded us in the car and
across country we went. I was beside myself because I had
always wanted to see the Pacific Ocean. I had dreamt about it
my whole life, and now we were on this journey.

And what a journey it was, too, my mom and four boys
crammed into our green '69 Chevy Impala. My oldest brother,
Steve, was 16 and had just gotten his driver's license. So he was
driving part of the way. That was an experience in itself.
Between me flicking him in the back of the head and all of us
fighting in the back seat, it was a hell of an experience. But that's
another story.

As soon as we got to Los Angeles, my Mom's youngest

29

sister, Terri, who was only two years older than me, but born on the same day, scooped me and my brothers up and drove us out to Laguna Beach. This was a beautiful little community and an internationally known art colony — a true Gallery Row. I mean there were galleries everywhere. Even I had heard about Laguna Beach, and anybody who knows anything about the place knew it had a rich history of art. I would come to find out later that many towns have their own sign of the Zodiac. Laguna's sign was the same as mine — Cancer, the water sign. So I felt really drawn to Laguna. To me, it was a magical place, a unique coastal city right on the Pacific Ocean.

Here was a kid who had dreamt about the ocean his entire life, and there it was, right in front of me. I immediately ran out into the water and just drank up the whole scene. Just as I looked back at Aunt Terri on the beach, a giant wave pounded me face first into the sand, rolling and tumbling me back onto the beach. Welcome to the Pacific Ocean! I jumped right back in, though — I was finally in a real ocean! Real salt water and sand. "I wonder what's under the surface," I thought to myself. So I started diving under to take a look. No sooner had I started doing this when I glanced out to sea and saw some huge creatures swimming no more than 100 yards off the beach, just past the waves. Wiping the salt water out my eyes, I focused in on them and, to my great astonishment, realized these were whales! These were the great California gray whales I had read so much about, migrating down the Pacific Coast to the warm breeding grounds of Mexico. Here was a kid who had been dying just to see the ocean, and then the greatest creatures on earth just happened to swim by, blowing in the water just a short swim away. What were the chances of something like that happening? I watched them swim on down the coast until I couldn't see them any longer and, when my head cleared, I realized I had just seen something I was meant to see. I believe that when someone sees a whale, he becomes a changed person. And I was definitely a changed person after these whales passed from my sight. It's hard to adequately describe the impact they had on me, except to say it was the most powerful thing I'd ever seen. I knew right then I would never forget it, and I didn't. Ironically, I would come back 10 years later and paint my first Whaling Wall less than 100 yards from where I had first seen these gray whales. Eventually, I moved to Laguna Beach and still live and work there in the summer.

We went back home to Detroit, and I continued my schooling. I found that the Pacific and the whales made such an impression on me that I started diving into libraries and trying to get my hands on anything I could find about whales. At that time, there really wasn't that much available. My art teacher, Mrs. Stevens, encouraged me with my paintings, which had begun to feature great whales, dolphins and the Pacific Ocean. My first "Above and Below" paintings were not very popular in 1971, but each year my artistic skill improved, and my appreciation for these creatures grew. It would be a few years before the movement to protect whales started gaining widespread attention. Greenpeace, of course, had started in the early '70s, and Jacques Cousteau would soon start producing his sea odysseys for television.

With Cousteau, the idea was that these intelligent animals were being hunted and needed protection, and Greenpeace reinforced that. Naturally, I got caught up in all of it because I had experienced whales first-hand and felt there had to be something I could do to help protect them as well.

The Politics of Painting the First Wall

For two years, I studied sculpture and painting in art school, the Center for Creative Studies. Primarily, I was painting classical figures and sculpting. The whole time, however, I found my mind and my palette leaning toward the ocean. I decided after these two very hard cold winters that my destiny was to be in California. I had to follow my dream, so, in 1976, at age 19, I decided to pack up the brushes in my old custom van and drive out to California.

The week I was getting ready to leave, one of my neighbors came by as my mom and I were sitting in front of the house talking. She said she had lived in California and told me, "You know, you may be a good artist in Detroit, but you'll never make it in California." Nice neighbor, eh? I guess she was jealous or something. What she didn't realize was that her kind words of encouragement only served to make me more determined. I recently ran into that same neighbor, who is now living in California in a rented house. She had read every newspaper article written about me by then, and had seen me on TV. She saw me in a grocery store and walked over and said "Wyland, you're doing so well. We're really proud of you!" I didn't have to say anything. My work spoke for itself.

Whale Tales

This was the first time I had ever moved out of my mom's home, and she was teary-eyed. She mentioned that we had some relatives living on the West Coast, but I decided I wanted to make it on my own. On the way out, I got waylaid in Colorado, fell in love with the Rocky Mountains and spent a few months there visiting my brother, Steve. But I really felt I belonged near the Pacific and moved on. I headed straight for Laguna Beach and got a little studio apartment, a tiny hole in the wall. This would be my studio, where I began selling my paintings.

Actually, I was doing small paintings and consigning them to an art gallery. I put together a body of work that was seen as very peculiar. I mean, paintings of whales? They weren't fast movers, to say the least. People liked the paintings and thought they were unique, but I think everyone, including my mom, thought I was going to starve to death. Whales? When they heard I was painting whales, I got a lot of funny looks. But somehow or other, I felt that if I was passionate about my art, eventually there would be a market for it. Even if there wasn't, if I felt good about it and was doing good paintings and could get by, I was comfortable with that. I wasn't really worried about being some super-rich artist. I was content having a roof over my head, some brushes and paint. That, to me, was being a professional artist.

I then started showing at the Sawdust Festival, which is a very famous art festival in Southern California. I would sit out there, paint and sell my own paintings from my booth. Believe me, it always happened this way: Whenever I had rent due or something like that, a painting would sell. Someone would see it just in time. This happened every month. I was living on Snickers bars and Hansens soda. My rent was $125 per month, and I was having trouble. The karma was extremely good, though, and, as appreciation for protecting the environment grew, so did people's appreciation for my work. I always felt something good would come of it sooner or later. Eventually, the well known Ruth Mayer Gallery started to handle my work.

As I painted more and more whales to make a living, I began to realize that something was driving me to look for larger canvasses. I was feeling contained, basically. Then, one day it hit me like a lightning bolt. "Hey, I've got to paint these things on walls," I said out loud to myself. I had done murals, lots of 'em. In a flash, it all clicked. If I was going to paint these animals as they really are, I should paint them lifesize. So I began to look for walls. I think I scouted the entire West Coast. I drove all the way from San Diego to San Francisco, charting and photographing walls. I think I was, and perhaps still am, the only person in the world driving around cities looking at ugly walls. But, like Dorothy looking for something over the rainbow, I couldn't see the perfect wall right in my own back yard. I mean it was right in front of me — so close I couldn't see it.

As I was coming home to Laguna, stuck in traffic, I spotted this giant wall on the highway. It was probably 600 feet long, right on the Pacific Coast Highway in North Laguna. When I saw it, I envisioned a pod of gray whales migrating off the Highway along with the traffic. Tens of thousands of people driving by couldn't possibly miss this wall; it was too public. They would see it and become inspired by the size, the beauty, the intelligence and the exceptional quality these animals have. I thought it would be a unique way to do something to help save whales. There was Greenpeace in their Zodiacs, and Cousteau with his beautiful inspiring films and documentaries. And now here was something I could do. From that day on, I called my work the Art of Saving Whales. I was only one artist, but with the ability to paint lifesize whales on a large scale, I thought I could get peoples' attention and impact them.

A friend of mine once wanted to write a piece for People Magazine, and they wrote him back asking him how painting a whale on a wall could possibly save whales. I came back and said it may very well be the only thing that can save the whales. Now that I look back on it, I believe that statement to be absolutely true. Without people being able to see these animals, either through public art or in the ocean, it'll be out of sight, out of mind. Good-bye whales.

So I had this great idea I would do a mural depicting the gray whale. This is where "above and below" started for me, on a lifesize scale. I had used the technique on some small canvases, but this is where I really had an opportunity to show the entire animal as they live and breathe above and below the ocean. This was very important to me because whales are like icebergs. You only see a small portion of them, and even that's very rare. I felt that if I could do the entire animal and educate the viewer below the surface, then people would be awestruck by what they saw.

Everything sort of came to me at once, as it usually does.

Whale Tales

The term "Whaling Wall" just came out of my mouth, simple, whales on walls, right? I didn't even think about the Wailing Wall in Jerusalem. But the symbolism is contagious; whales are very special, some of God's greatest creatures. Why not worship whales? Man's long history of thinking of animals as being there only for his use is one earth's greatest tragedies. Whales are a product of beauty worthy of protection. Given the history of whaling, the Whaling Walls are a celebration of living whales. The walls are gathering places for people who care about them.

I had done murals since '72, including many in Southern California. The first showed a diver in a wild ocean on the side of a dive shop called Black Barts. Then I did a sea captain on a seafood restaurant, and a mural with musical notes on the side of The Golden Bear in Huntington Beach. But these and other murals had all been commissioned by the owners of the walls I was to paint. This time no request had come forth; I was the one initiating the work. It would be the first time I would not charge for a mural. That didn't matter, though. I had done a lot of things to make a living, and this was the first time I had wanted to give something back. I also saw it as a great challenge, and I felt the need to bring attention to these great creatures. At that point, I decided that in order to proceed I'd have to find out who owned the wall. I went to Greenpeace right off, thinking they might help me because they were involved with saving whales. They had an office in Huntington Beach, where I met with the director and his colleagues and showed them a rendering. They loved it immediately and proceeded to find out whose approval I needed and who might be willing to help pay for paint and provide equipment. We talked to Cal Trans—the State of California Transportation Department. They thought it was a terrific idea, but they had no funding. So they tried to get the blessing of the state's Public Art Projects. There were several murals already in LA, on the freeway and things like that, but this would be the largest one in the area. At this point, I had no concept of the bureaucracy involved with a project like this. I never dreamed that to paint a public mural like this would require me to become embroiled in a three-year quagmire of politics. How could I have known? I was just an artist trying to do something to help whales. I know now it was naive, and call me idealistic, but I sort of expected people to help me with this vision.

Whale Tales

Greenpeace eventually gave up, threw in the towel. This was a good indication of the level of politics involved. Greenpeace? International Giant-Killers? They don't normally give up. We had to attend countless city meetings. Cal Trans backed us initially and were supportive, but the City was where it started getting ugly. The mayor of the City of Laguna Beach was opposed to it, for reasons no one was ever sure of. To this day, I think it was because it wasn't his idea, a situation I still run into on occasion. I had to agree that this was a unique project. There were no public murals in Laguna — a city rich in art history — no indoor murals, no outdoor murals. To me it was a natural. I mean, here's a coastal city; here's the ocean; here are the gray whales, the state marine mammal for Christ's sake. There was no better place; it was just common sense. I learned pretty quickly, though, that common sense doesn't always get you there. I was about to learn that in order for me to publicly share the Art of Saving Whales, I would first have to learn the Politics of Painting Murals.

First and foremost, I had the blessing of the owner of the wall, Cal Trans. BUT, only if the City agreed first. Okay, I went to the City, accompanied by Greenpeace, who made a tremendous presentation. Most of the officials liked it, but the mayor didn't. He managed somehow to convince some of the city council members it was not a good idea for Laguna. Then it was my turn to try and convince the council members. It was the first time I had ever done anything like this, and I was anything but a slick lobbyist. I was an artist, not known for my speaking ability, a long-haired kind of New Age thinker trying to deal with all of these "suits." I didn't buy a suit. I wasn't ever going to wear a suit. But I did try to play the game. I lobbied some of the other council members who had been warm towards the rendering, but they — for reasons the public would never know — couldn't make a decision right away.

Anyway, we went to meetings for two years. Yes, over two years of meetings. And they kept putting it off, putting it off, putting it off. Finally, a group called the North Laguna Community Association — a group of older people, much older people, were also having trouble with the City because they wanted to get a traffic light installed right next to the wall I wanted to paint. Ironically, the city was starting to warm up to my idea when all of a sudden this association of very experienced and vocal senior citizens decided they would use my wall as a political vehicle to get their light. They strongly opposed the wall, and it became a big stinking controversy. I went to one of the association's meetings to explain the details of the mural. This was the final approval we needed to get the city council to vote in our favor. But it was a complete set-up. The association shot the project down from every angle possible, and then from some angles that had nothing to do with anything possible. Their aging imaginations kicked in that night and just ran away with them, I guess. All I knew was that I had wanted to paint something beautiful for this city. Instead, things had become very, very ugly.

It came down to one final city council meeting where three of the five council members told me point blank they were in favor of the mural and that it was going to pass. When it came time to make the final presentation to the council, there was a lot of really emotional testimony as to why this mural was important. A couple of North Laguna Community Association members testified as well, saying "Hey, this Wyland's not even from Laguna Beach. He wasn't born here," that kind of crap. You know, "Why doesn't he paint the whales being harpooned?" I couldn't believe my ears on that one. The idea of painting living whales didn't appeal to them. They wanted more action — they wanted some harpooning! Basically, they were pulling straws out of a hat. The bottom line — I was stabbed right in the middle of the back and heart. The city council voted against it — all of them. It had been three years since I had first approached the City for approval. I was absolutely committed to this wall and had spent every dime I had, roughly $20,000, just to survive. It wasn't easy to paint and earn a living when I was constantly attending meetings and making presentations. I was totally dejected, three years of my life down the drain.

Heartbroken, I walked out of the City Hall building and started toward my car. Suddenly, Tom Klingenmeier, a reporter from a local paper called *The Tides and Times*, walked up, put his arm around me and said, "Look, Wyland, I've been following this for three years, and I gotta tell you — I'm from Chicago and they have murals there that were very well received. Don't give up. This thing is worth fighting for. Eventually, it's going to happen. Stay in there. . . stay on it."

Tom, who today I count as one of my closest friends, had

indeed covered this Laguna mural controversy since the beginning. I had interviewed with him many times. In fact, after the first meeting with the council three years before, he told me, "I can't believe anyone would be against this thing." Through his newspaper column, he had stood by the project start to finish. I valued his opinion and appreciated the encouragement he was trying to give me. But at that point, I had given up and thrown in the towel.

I was so shattered that it took me a couple of days to recover. This was the worst kind of treachery there was, as far as I was concerned. After being told, "Hey, you've got my vote," and "no problem," by three of the council members, all of whom gave me friendly slaps on the back the very morning of my final presentation — it was just too much.

Klingenmeier, however, called me a couple of more times and said, "You know, the more I think about this thing, the more I think it's worth the fight. I think if you find another wall, the City will go for it. Less than 48 hours later, I decided I would just find another site, and that's exactly what I did. There was another wall on Pacific Coast Highway, which I had, in fact, seen before I had seen the wall that was shot down by the City. It was on private property, the Hotel

The Politics of Painting the First Wall

Laguna, one of the oldest hotels and historic sites in Laguna. So I approached the owner, who was very receptive.

It was an awful looking retaining wall, about 140 feet long and 26 feet high, and I figured the City might not care that much about it. Plus, I had learned something about the process of approvals, so I gave it another try. Much to my surprise, the City said "yes" immediately. They were sick of looking at me, I guess. Either that or I wore 'em out. This time, I needed permission from the Laguna Design Review, whom I didn't know, and from the Laguna Arts Council. I wasn't worried about the Arts council because they were already for it. And I didn't have to deal with the North Laguna Beach Community Association again because this wall was downtown. I had another asset on this one as well — Tom Klingenmeier. He had himself another story to write.

The vote among the Design Review was close: two in favor, two opposed, one on the fence. The guy on the fence was a guy named Dan Kenney, and I remember him staring at me, trying to decide if he should really do this. He looked at me for a long time and finally said, "I have reservations, and I'm not sure I should do this. . . but okay."

I was ecstatic, to put it mildly, and thanked the review

board profusely, especially Dan. To this day, every time I run into him, he reminds me: "I gave you the vote that gave you your first wall, you know."

Finally, we had won. We had won! The next morning, I was down there at 7:00. Tom was there, and there was this high school kid named Matt Fahee just hanging out. It was their tough luck. Like Tom Sawyer, I put both of them to work. As I was mixing all the paint, I had Tom call the scaffolding company to find out how much it would cost. I couldn't afford to scaffold the whole wall, so I got three sections and piled them on top of each other. Unfortunately, they only raised me so high, and I had to leave the top undone, having reached as high as I could. I just didn't have enough money to rent any more scaffolding. I needed to spend the rest of what I had on the paint.

Sinclair Paint gave me half off, and I traded a painting and the rest of my cash for the other half. I had, like, six bucks left. We loaded all the paint in the back of my pickup truck, which had no tailgate on it. Having just painted the bottom section of the wall, we were hungry and went down to Jack in the Box in South Laguna. When we were done, we piled into the pickup and quickly pulled out onto the highway to head back to the wall. Everything would have been fine if it weren't for that big dip at the exit. When I hit it without a tailgate, all 200 gallons of paint, in five-gallon cans, went flying and tumbling out of the back of the truck and all over the highway. I had created a "Blue Laguna."

This paint was a teal blue, not a color you'd normally find, especially blasted all over the Pacific Coast Highway. Cars were running over the cans; the paint was flying 20 feet in the air. Before I could pull over, I had trailed a ten-foot-wide strip a quarter of a mile long. Cars were racing through it, splashing it up on Rolls Royces, Porsches, Mercedes — there are a lot of these in Laguna Beach. People were jumping out and screaming, "My car! My car!" I was sitting there watching in horror. I was out of money, and I had no stinking paint — I was a dead man. The City was already watching me like a hawk, and I had messed up part of their community one day after they had given me their approval.

I did, however, see a couple of cans still intact as they lay on their sides in the middle of the road. So I got out of the truck and tried to look inconspicuous as I salvaged them. I reached down and picked up the paint cans, and someone yelled, "Hey Wyland, you're supposed to be painting the wall!"

I scurried back to my truck to get out of sight when three fire trucks, sirens wailing, pulled up to hose the mess down, even though most of the paint was drying. I made a deal with one of the fireman who figured out I was the culprit, when he saw the bed of my truck covered in the same shade of blue that adorned the highway. I told him I would give him a painting if he wouldn't tell anyone.

Fortunately, things aren't always as bad as they seem. I think at this point the City really felt sorry for me, so they didn't harass me. They knew I was the one who spilled the paint, but I think they really felt bad. They also knew I had my entire life tied up in this paint, and I had spilled it all over the highway. Then, when I explained the story to Sinclair, they gave me more paint, enough in fact, to finish the wall. Believe it or not, "Blue Laguna" is still visible on Pacific Coast Highway. I see it every time I drive by.

I painted with real passion because I had a mission. The wall now has a mother gray whale and her calf making their way past Laguna Beach on their migration from the Bering Sea to Baja, Mexico. I was really ready after three years of working to obtain approval for the work, and I think I painted one of my most beautiful murals because of the release from this frustration. It turned out to be a major art event for the city as I painted. The crowds were enormous. People were pulling their cars over and creating huge traffic jams. And, that's what I wanted. This was an event; this was a vehicle to show people how beautiful these animals are and that they are worthy of protection. That's when I decided I would do 100 Whaling Walls. I thought if I could make that big of an impact with one mural, what could I do if I painted 100? About halfway through the painting, that figure just sort of slipped out of my mouth, and the press jumped on it.

It took me 30 days to complete the wall, exactly 30 days. I had to get the scaffolding back before then or I would have had to pay extra. Many of the people originally opposed to the mural were the first ones to commend it. They said they had no idea how beautiful it was going to be. The entire city embraced it, and I went from goat to hero. I had taken on the bureaucrats and didn't give up. Most artists would have thrown in the towel and said forget it, especially when there was no money in it. I did this wall all out of pocket and from my heart and was so far in the hole that it took me two years to recover financially.

When the wall was finished, I had to rent three rooms at the hotel so my family could attend the dedication. The rooms overlooking the Hotel Laguna parking lot had previously been $30. Ocean view rooms were $40. After I painted the mural, they raised the price of the room with the parking lot view to the same as the Ocean view rooms. It was an ugly parking lot view before, but now the guests could gaze out their windows and see a technicolor Whaling Wall. It actually cost me $30 more for those rooms because I painted the mural. And, at the time, that was a lot of money for me.

Although he gave me approval to paint the parking lot wall, the guy who owned the hotel at the time turned out to be a real pain in the ass throughout the project. He could have provided some meals or something, I thought. Here he was getting a beautiful mural in his parking lot for free that was going to enhance his hotel for years. He was getting media from all over the world, free media: Hotel Laguna, Hotel Laguna. But he wouldn't even throw out some cheeseburgers. On the day I finished the mural, the sun was setting and I was feeling really good. This guy walks out of his hotel, drunk, completely bombed out of his mind, and said, "Well, this looks beautiful. I understand you have quite a bit of your own money in this?"

"Yes I do," I replied.

"Well, I can help you out with that. How much do you have in it?"

"Oh, I probably have about $10,000 in it," I said, knowing that I had spent much more during the three years it took to see the mural through.

"Well," he said again, "I can definitely help you out with that."

He avoided me like the plague for the next three years. I mean if he saw me, he ran. He never did help me out. But that's okay. The hotel is under new ownership now, and they're very supportive of my work. Four years later, the city asked me to come to City Hall — the same people who had earlier shot me down — to give me a resolution for my work and ask me to do another mural. In an indirect manner, they tried to explain their earlier denial as a situation where everyone was scared of change. A blank wall is frightening. And believe me, for an artist, a blank wall is frightening, but some people have vision. For others, new things are hard to accept. I knew this wall would be a tremendous piece of public art and eventually a landmark. When I was painting it, there it was for them to see. When they could visualize it, they became enthusiastic.

I guess it's all about the fear of the unknown. I myself have seen a lot of horrible murals, and how were they to know this wouldn't be another one? I believe everything happens for a reason, and this Whaling Wall was meant to be from the time I took that first swim off Laguna Beach and saw my first gray whale. The mural is still there and has become one of Southern California's favorite landmarks. For me, it marked the start of a much greater work — the first of 100 Whaling Walls around the world. For Laguna Beach, I think it might have marked the beginning of a new medium in that city's art history.

The Politics of Painting the First Wall

3

Chumming for Whales

...If the oceans are calling, it must be the song of the whales...

Wyland

*I*t was 1982 and I was excitedly preparing to go on my first whale expedition to the San Ignacio Lagoon. The area is a renowned breeding ground for the California Gray Whales, who for millions of years have migrated to the lagoons to give birth. This made it very easy for local whalers, who for centuries would just wait until the lagoons filled up with hundreds of whales, then herd them up and harpoon the babies before the larger parents and escorts could make their way to the offspring and rescue them.

Often, fierce battles would ensue as the whales would ram the whaling vessels in self-defense, thus earning the whales the nickname of the "Hardheaded Whales." Ironically, and fortunately, the handle has since changed to "The Friendly Gray Whales." They've earned this title because they now literally come over to the lagoon skiffs and bring their calves over so you can touch them. This is what I mean when I tell people the whaling industry is being replaced with the whale-watching industry.

In any case, I'd heard these stories for years and, finally, was getting a chance to go down and see these whales first-hand. The California gray whale was the first I had ever laid eyes on as a youth and, to me, this was going to be an experience of a lifetime. We were to leave that evening at midnight, and it would take three or four days just to get there, and three or four more to get back. It had all the makings of a fantastic voyage, and everything was perfect — except for one thing. Until now, not too many people have known this, but I am very prone to. . . seasickness.

Yes, I'm okay near the shore. But just a little way out, and I turn as green as a shamrock. In the water, under it, no problem. But you better have a mop and pail aboard if you want to take me out where the big swells can have their way with me. I knew exactly what I was getting myself into. Ten days at sea for me was like. . . well, it's indescribable, not a very pretty sight. But I wanted to see these whales so bad that none of this mattered. At least I didn't think it did.

Chumming for Whales

Now, with these kind of trips, there's a lot of camaraderie beforehand — drinking, partying and carrying on. Most of the guys who were going I knew, and most of them, like me, were going to San Ignacio for the first time. Several of them were whale artists as well, friends of mine and established in the art community of Northern California. There was J.D. Mahew, who has been painting whales most of his life; "Bird" Baker, a big burly sea captain kind of a guy who you'd never guess was a fine artist by looking at him; and Jerry Glover, a well known West Coast sculptor of whales and dolphins.

We had all met at the harbor in San Diego and, naturally, had a huge dinner while we drank and laughed, talked about whales and exchanged sea stories. In our revelry we drank numerous mugs of draft beer and ate lots of fish, lots and lots of fish. We boarded the vessel at midnight. It was a 110-foot motor boat, a fishing rig called "Searcher." It was pitch black as we shoved off toward the mouth of the harbor, and I was already feeling a little queasy. My mind and stomach were both thinking, "What if I. . ." Anyone who has ever had the sensation of being seasick will appreciate this.

Whale Tales

Although it had only been several minutes, it seemed as if we had motored out toward the dark depths for hours before we finally turned south for Mexico. Most everyone was down below continuing their fish stories and drinking, but I was already topside gulping at the fresh air as the currents and swells became worse and worse, rocking the boat from side to side. I had been on boats before on Lake Michigan and was well aware of my Achilles Heel stomach. I had long before graduated from Dramamine to a seasick patch, which was stuck to my neck like an inflation valve on an inner tube. I was waiting for that baby to kick in but, by then, it was too late. As Wayne and Garth would say, I was getting ready to "hurl" when I sensed the huge body of Bird Baker standing next to me. Now Bird was a character right out of a novel — a virtual giant, six-feet-five and 300 pounds, with red and gray hair and a red beard, a huge gut and a loud gravelly voice. I'm not sure if he was swaying because of the motion of the boat or because of the quart of whiskey he held in his hand, but I had a hard time focusing on him.

It didn't matter if I could see him very well. I knew where he was when one of the hams he had for hands grabbed me around the waist and squeezed my stomach so hard I could barely breathe. It was weird, but he farted real loud as he squeezed my belly. I've never figured that one out.

"WHAT THE HELL'S THE MATTER WITH YOU?" he bellowed in my face, turning it green with a big waft of whisky breath. I think most of the libation was dripping down his beard onto his massive chest.

"I'm sick," I said weakly.

"OH BULLSHIT! YOU AIN'T SEASICK. COME ON, HAVE A DRINK."

"No, Bird," I said weakly, "I'm really sick, and you're making me sicker. Get lost."

He just stood there swaying and pouring whiskey down his mouth and chin for a few minutes, looking me over and trying to think of something else to say. I guess he figured it out and decided he didn't want to get puked on. As he staggered back to the ladder leading below deck, he shouted over his shoulder, "WELL, OKAY, GOOD LUCK. . . CHUCK."

Good luck? Good luck with what? Did he hope I wouldn't get any on the deck? Did he think I might recover and come down and drink with him and the boys? Whatever crossed his inebriated mind, he wasn't hanging around. He had just nauseated me further and gone on his merry way. Thanks, Bird.

In the whale-puking business, they call it chumming. I was staggering at this point, looking for a good place to hang my head over the side of the Searcher. Suddenly, the boat's name had taken on a new meaning to me — I, too, had become a searcher. It was cold, but I didn't want to ruin my jacket so I took it off, laid it on the deck and stuck my head over the side to survey the situation. The ocean was heaving up and down, and I was just about to do the same when the captain of the boat comes down from the steering cavity and says, "What in the hell are you doing? You sick? Hell, we just got out here. It doesn't get any calmer than this!"

Thanks, captain — just what I needed to hear. I proceeded to chum the water for, oh, about two hours. Each time I thought I was finished, I made an attempt to go below and find my bunk. But, each time, I had to turn around when I was half-way there and scurry back to my spot in the aft part of the Searcher. It was really cold and by then raining with a strong wind just for atmosphere. Like a wet rat, I was puking all over myself, the wind blowing it right back in my face. It was a nightmare, a scene right out of a movie. After a dozen attempts to go below, I had sort of given up and just sat down near my jacket at my post. By the time sun came up, I had thrown up everything but my nuts. I must have lost 10 pounds.

Finally, I guess I decided I'd had enough. I went down below expecting to get sick again, but somehow made it to my bunk. I had to sleep. My bunk was on the top, and Jerry Glover was fast asleep, snoring loudly in the rack below me. I hoped I wouldn't throw up all over this poor slumbering bastard.

I lay there, crunched up, with the ceiling only inches from my face and feeling horrible. A chunk got caught in my throat, and I was ready to go again. No way I was going back up topside. I just said "screw it" and tried to hit a tiny sink from where I was lying. The whale chum hit the mirror, the floor — it was terrible. I repeated this two more times, too weary to leave my bunk. Jerry just snored away, not the least bit disturbed. At last, I laid my head down and passed out from exhaustion.

Within minutes, the below deck loudspeaker, also a few

inches from my face, crackled and a loud voice boomed, "BREAKFAST TIME. . . BREAKFAST TIME." I jolted straight up, banging my swollen head on the ceiling. Jerry, of course, popped up and rushed out to eat his fill of what is usually my favorite meal of the day. Just as I started to doze off again, the loudspeaker erupted again, "LAST CALL FOR BREAKFAST."

I forced myself to roll out and climb out of the berthing area. Topside, the mess decks were full of hungry men chowing down like they hadn't eaten in years. Something about being on the ocean makes people really hungry. Not me — it was making me sick. I had placed two seasick patches on either side of my neck and was praying that one of them might work. I'll never do a commercial for a seasick patch company. Before long, the smacking sound of my buddies devouring their breakfast got to me, and I returned to my post and continued the chumming. It was only the first morning! This scene repeated itself continuously every day on the way to our destination and then back again. Thanks to the mess cook, the crew and guests of the Searcher were very well fed the entire trip. Thanks to me, so were half the fish along the Pacific Coast.

Chumming for Whales

After what seemed like two years, we came upon a small island where we disembarked to do some hiking and photography. I immediately fell on the beach and kissed the ground, filling my mouth and moustache with sand. I didn't care, though. I was on dry ground, and my stomach got a reprieve. While we were hiking, I almost inadvertently stepped on the head of a 17-foot elephant seal. The thing reared up and scared the shit out of me. I ran over 10 people trying to get away. But it was okay, the seal was just as startled as I was. We hiked for a couple of hours, taking pictures, and I did some drawings of the elephant seals. When we reboarded the Searcher, I was feeling queasy but much better. I knew we were getting close to the gray whales.

San Ignacio Lagoon was everything I thought it would be. There were whales everywhere. They were spy-hopping, where they stick their heads out of the water to look around, and riding waves like giant surfers into the lagoon. Pulling into the lagoon, I noticed 20-30 whales and their calves following us like puppies. I forgot all about being seasick. It was all just so incredible, whales everywhere, all kinds of behavior, blowing all over the surface. It was tremendous.

Whale Tales

We dropped down into these small boats called skiffs and just drifted in the lagoon. Within seconds, a mother swam over to us with her baby. I'll never forget this as long as I live. The mother came right up to the skiff and lifted the baby up to us. I reached my hand over the bow of the skiff, and the baby nuzzled my hand. My God, I had actually touched a whale! The mother sort of rolled over, and I started scratching both of them. At one point, I had my whole arm inside the mother's mouth, scratching her tongue. It was just incredible the amount of control these animals had. I mean, two feet away, they never even bumped the skiff, which was racing with the current. This went on for hours, various whales coming over to us and letting us touch and scratch them. It was strange to think that in this famous whaling lagoon where countless whales had not long before been slaughtered, the same species was swimming up to us and offering their babies to touch.

As an artist, I remembered every detail. I didn't know they had all those barnacles and whale lice. I remember how their skin felt and their eyes — their little eyelids, the little hair follicles around them, hairs on their chin. They had individual markings, scratches and things like that. And they had individual personalities. Some were very friendly and curious; others were shy and stand-offish, kind of like us. For the first time I started thinking of whales as individuals instead of as a group. Some of them had underbites; some had overbites. It was an invaluable, close-up look at the details of their anatomy, a thrilling experience that taught me things I still use in my paintings today. I was a changed person. Even my own physical appearance had changed — 10 days of chumming will do that to you.

4
Eye to Eye with the Humpbacks

...Whales leave footprints on the surface of the ocean..

Wyland

*T*here may be some who think I was an overnight success as an artist, fortunate to have come along about the same time environmental art was starting to gain popularity. But nothing could have been farther from the truth. As a matter of fact, I was the prototype "starving artist" until the mid to late '80s, when, finally, I started to earn a little money from my depictions of whales swimming in their natural habitats.

I had enjoyed some success in Laguna Beach at the Sawdust Festival, but it wasn't exactly overwhelming. I had been studying and painting whales and other marine life for years and, by the end of 1979, had decided to move to Maui and set up a little studio in Lahaina. I was aware through my research that Lahaina was one of the world's most historic whaling villages, and that the great humpback whales migrated there from Alaska each winter to mate and calve. I'd never been to the Hawaiian Islands, but I was an artist who had found his subject. So, in early 1980, I packed my bags and moved to Maui to get closer to these magnificent creatures, with the hope that spending time with them would enhance my work.

Lahaina was a spot unique on the earth. Its lush, laid-back character was a perfect compliment to the warm clear waters the humpbacks had enjoyed off its shore for thousands of years. You could actually see the whales frolicking a couple of hundred yards from downtown Lahaina as if they were at summer camp. Only this was winter. I had hardly any money by the time I paid my way over to Hawaii, but I knew immediately upon arriving in Lahaina that something more powerful than my curiosity had drawn me to the place. The whales were there. I was there. Now all I had to do was set up a studio and start painting.

I found the studio in a loft right on Front Street. It was really tiny, and it cost $150 a month, more than I had in my pocket. But I had the "luck of the whale" in me and had always had the uncanny good fortune of selling a painting whenever I found myself down to my last nickel. And that's exactly what happened. I made enough to move in and get started. I had a little futon I would roll up during the day so I could make room for my easel and my canvasses. My meals consisted largely of Snicker's bars cut up in three parts — one for breakfast, one for lunch and one for dinner. I soaked off the oil paint each evening in the jacuzzi at the Lahaina Shores Hotel down the street. This was a far cry from overnight success, but I was very productive during this period, excited to be a working artist living with my subjects in Lahaina.

One day I was painting like crazy when I heard a knock at the door. Slightly irritated at being disrupted, I slung the door open and found a man and woman who turned out to be Mark and Debbie Ferrari, world-renowned whale researchers who had been studying the humpback for many years and had made tremendous progress researching these whales off Maui. They said hello and told me they had become aware of my work and wanted to drop by and introduce themselves. They wanted to invite me to go out with them the next morning and swim with the whales.

Needless to say, I was ecstatic. They seemed very pleased

at my reaction and proceeded to tell me they supported what I was doing with my art. They also indicated that the whales in my paintings were not exactly right. It was their idea — and I agreed wholeheartedly with them — that if I were to dive under the surface and actually swim with the whales, I would have an opportunity to learn about their true essence and anatomy.

That night I was too excited to sleep. This was better than I had ever imagined. I liked these people. I was a starving artist; they were starving researchers; and we all three loved whales and wanted to do something about their preservation. As eager as I was, there was no way I could ever prepare myself for what would happen the next day — a day that would change my life and my work.

We met at the pier in Lahaina early in the morning and headed down the north coast of Maui toward Kihei and Wailea. We saw humpbacks the whole way, and I was kind of wondering when Mark was going to stop his Zodiac so we could get in the water with them. But he and Debbie were looking for "Daisy," a female Humpback they had seen in the Hawaiian waters year after year. They explained to me that whales don't particularly like divers because of the bubbles from their oxygen tanks, so I had my snorkeling gear ready to go. Finally, they spotted Daisy and her calf and steered the inflatable in her direction.

At that time, the Ferrari's research consisted largely of determining which whales were coming to Maui every year and which ones were calving. They weren't tagging them or anything like that, just photo-identifying them. I had my camera with me and was really honored to be part of the research team. But my role, both in my mind and in those of my new mates, was to swim with the whales. Debbie and I slipped into the water to do just that when we saw three whales on the surface. We waited for the whales to dive so Debbie could see their "footprints" in the water. This is called "sounding," which allowed her to tell pretty much which direction they were heading. The trick now, she said, was to get a little closer and just wait until the whales took an interest and swam over to us.

It was a perfect Maui day with 150-foot visibility, which means crystal clear water. Below us the ocean was deep blue, and we couldn't see the bottom. I dove down about 10 feet and leveled off looking for what I expected to be their huge shapes. I was suspended in a pyramid of light cascading down into a laser-sharp point below me. The first thing I noticed was the sound. It was the beautiful, haunting song of the humpback. It's hard to characterize, but it was like an orchestra of cows and birds and parakeets — the most extraordinary sounds, like nothing I had ever heard. I knew the whales were communicating with one another, and wondered if they were talking about us.

Then, after what seemed like a couple of seconds, I saw something massive materialize before me, and I suddenly realized it was a mother and her calf swimming straight at me. At that very moment, I had to surface and get another breath of air. I wanted to stay down, but I had to breathe. My heart racing, I inhaled the fresh air and went right back down as fast as I could. The two whales were still there, not the least alarmed that I had to go to the surface and breathe, which they themselves had to do. They then slowly started swimming right over to me. Despite their size, they looked like dancers in a ballet, gliding their bodies in slow graceful motions through the crystalline cathedral of light.

I was so entranced that I didn't realize I was swimming toward them as well. The calf was staying very close to its mother as the three of us almost collided. At the very last moment, the mother deftly raised her long flipper over my head to avoid hitting me. It was so incredible — she was totally in tune with where I was and the distance between us. She appeared to have sensed that her awesome size could have damaged me, and she went out of her way to dodge me.

It was nothing short of mesmerizing to be that close to these great mammals. We had found Daisy and her calf, and I could see both of them from head to tail. I could see everything. But the image that still burns in my memory were the eyes. I was probably 50 feet away from them when they first started swimming toward me. As they drew closer — 20 feet, 10 feet, five feet — the mother's eye got real big. The great creature looked right into my eyes and right into my soul. I felt like I was looking into her soul, too, the soul of a very ancient being. I could see every detail of her eyes, all the colors. The whites of the eyes were a white-yellow. Her calf was right above her and appeared to want to swim to me and play. They both looked excited to see us, and I think they recognized Debbie.

I had to do everything I could to contain myself and not touch these animals. In fact, I wanted to stay down with them so bad I almost forgot to breathe. Fortunately, common sense kicked in and I shot up to the surface. At this point, they were swimming past me, and I noticed a third whale, their escort, trailing behind and executing a beautiful bubble blow. I had painted this very scene from photos and films from Cousteau, but now I was living it and watching it unfold right in front of me.

It was a phenomenal learning experience for an artist. I remember being surprised by their great girth and oversized flippers. They were mostly black with some gray. Their dorsal fins were different from each other's, one having more white markings than the other. I made mental notes of everything.

I realized that we were out of our element, and they were in theirs. They'd been here 40 million years, and it was very special to have them show themselves to me. It was like the mother was showing me her calf so I could take the vision and share it with others. At least that's how I felt about it.

To my utter amazement, the whales turned around and returned to swim with us for another 20 minutes before moving on. I didn't have to swim back to the boat, I walked on top of the water. Both Mark and Debbie had huge grins on their faces; they knew what this meant to me. It was the best gift I had ever received, and still is.

This was the beginning of my diving with whales. I still go out with Mark and Debbie every winter and try to dive with the humpbacks. In fact, to this day, every winter when these whales come to Hawaii, I come to Hawaii. And when they leave in the spring, I leave, too.

I think it's important that I remain close to Mark and Debbie. Scientists and artists don't always get along, but they need to find more ways to work together. Isn't it interesting that it was an ancient mammal of the sea that helped bring us together? That keeps me balanced, even now. I spend time in the water, and I spend time in the studio. It's the best of both worlds. I continue to dive with whales all over the world. But that first time, eye to eye with the humpbacks, was just like a first love — you always remember.

5

Judge Saves Wyland's Whaling Wall

...Some have said, "How can a painting of a whale on a wall save them?"
I believe it may very well be the only thing that can...

WYLAND

I was making my way back to my studio in Lahaina after painting my first Whaling Wall in Laguna Beach, stopping in Honolulu to look for a wall I could paint in Hawaii. It was late 1981, and I was already experienced at this, having spent a lot of time traveling up and down California's Pacific Coast Highway looking for walls to paint. Sometimes it's hard to really see everything when you're driving at the same time. So I figured the best way to go would be by city bus. At that time, it only cost 25 cents to ride the bus all over Oahu. You could get a transfer ticket and get off and on, or you could ride all day if you wanted, which was ideal for me. I could let them do the driving, and I could do the looking.

Anyone who has ever ridden The Bus in Hawaii knows

what an experience it can be. The people who climb aboard come from all walks of life and ethnic backgrounds — tourists, working professionals, schoolchildren, senior citizens, politicians, construction workers, and a hodgepodge of characters I swear are from other planets. Venice Beach has nothing on Honolulu when it comes to strange characters.

I boarded The Bus on this day with two large bags of luggage, which they don't normally allow you to do, and took a seat near the front right side where I could see out the front of the vehicle as well as the side. I had spotted a few interesting walls on my circle-island tour when the bus approached Waikiki on Ala Moana Boulevard. I was gazing out the windows when suddenly to my right appeared this tremendous wall that looked to be 20 stories high and as long as a football field. As we drew closer, I knew this was to be my perfect Whaling Wall.

I got so excited I automatically reached up and pulled the cord that signalled the driver to stop the bus at the next stop, which was still a quarter a mile away. I told the driver I had to get off right then, and I suppose he saw by the look on my face that I meant it. So he stopped the bus, which they don't normally do, and I threw my bags into the street and ran up to the wall. It sounds strange, but I get very excited about large blank walls, and I just stood in front of this one and smiled. It was not only the right shape and size, it was right on Ala Moana Boulevard between the Ilikai Hotel and Kaiser Hospital. The passengers of every car, bus, taxi or limousine who entered Waikiki would pass right by the mural, and every boat off Waikiki would be able to see it from the water. It was. . . a 10.

Immediately, I had a vision of an entire pod of humpback whales swimming across the length of the wall. There was a large tower section that was very high, and I saw a lifesize humpback breaching up into it. I stopped looking for walls on the spot and rushed back to Maui and did a rendering. It would be two years before I felt comfortable presenting it because of my fear that someone would say no. But, when I got up the courage, I flew over to talk to the manager of the Ilikai Marina Building.

The lady's name was Marge McDowell, a beautiful, fiery woman who had no idea who I was or that I was going to barge into her office unannounced with a plan that would eventually make her building famous.

"Hi, my name's Wyland; I'm an artist; I paint murals;

and I'd like to show you something," I said boldly, walking past her and unrolling the rendering on her desk. I had shown the rendering to some people on the beach earlier that day, and sand spilled all over her desk.

I was having an anxiety attack about receiving a negative reaction from her. But, to my complete surprise and relief, she loved the rendering and loved the idea. "This is fantastic," she said. "We'll need to show it to the board, but I don't think there will be a problem. That side of the building is such an eyesore anyway. It might even improve the value of the building."

A few months later, we had a meeting with the Ilikai Marina Board. Again, I was very nervous. When I painted my first Whaling Wall in Laguna Beach, I had seen how a proposal, no matter how much support it had, could be held up or endangered by the smallest of dissents. But, like Marge, most of the board members were enthusiastically in favor of me doing the wall. I was ecstatic because we had passed the first, and what should have been the most important, hurdle in gaining approval for the mural. Actually, we went through several months of presentations to various agencies and community groups, with each one being very positive and supportive. In fact, John Hillerman, who played "Higgins" on *Magnum P.I.*, attended the Waikiki Neighborhood Board meeting and spoke on my behalf. John, a good friend of mine who owned several of my pieces, lived in Waikiki and was member of the neighborhood board. He told them this mural was going to be very important to the state. His impact was very impressive, and the board voted unanimously in favor of the mural.

This was supposed to be the last hurdle, but I got a call a few days later and was asked if I would mind meeting with a group I had never heard of called "The Outdoor Circle." It was not required that we obtain permission from this group; we had all the permits and permission we needed. But I felt so good about all of the support I had received that I decided, as a goodwill gesture, to meet with the Circle. It wasn't until later I was informed that this was a group of mostly rich, powerful older women who for decades had opposed outdoor public art. Their big claim to fame had been an early victory in keeping billboard advertising out of Hawaii, a noble enterprise, but one that had taken place over 50 years ago. They have since become one of the most powerful lobbies in the state of Hawaii, keeping a vigilant watch for anything they feel could be even tenuously tied to out-door advertising. Unfortunately, by the time I came on the scene, their collective mission had become so dogmatic and distorted that they had anointed themselves, quite unoffi-cially, as the watchdog assigned to protect Hawaii from in-appropriate public art. The bottom line was that murals were definitely taboo.

I was told of the Outdoor Circle's political clout and money, and that they had been around a long time. But I felt I could somehow win them over to my side. I was still living in Lahaina and working hard to survive as an artist. A girl-friend of mine, Cheryl Fitzharris, was visiting me from Whiterock, Canada, where I had previously painted a Whal-ing Wall. The week before we were to fly to Honolulu to meet the Circle, some friends of mine, Gale and Kathy Notestone, decided they wanted to take us to Haleakala Cra-ter to watch the sunrise. It sounded like a good idea, and Cheryl was excited about it, so we decided to go. Well, we got up there and nearly froze watching the sun come up. Then Gale got this bright idea we all should hike through Haleakala — all the way through. It sounded like fun; be-sides, it was so cold that walking sounded like a darn good idea at the time. The only problem was that we weren't really dressed for it — we weren't wearing cold-weather clothes and didn't have the right shoes. Cheryl, who was a beautiful model, very glamorous, was wearing high heels. She was graceful and sweet and just a perfect companion, willing to do her best at anything. We said, "Why not?"

Anyone who has hiked Haleakala knows the weather ranges up there from freezing ice cold to searing heat and dust. It's also a 13-14 mile hike. Obviously, I don't count myself as one of those who knew any of this beforehand. We proceeded down the crater and, after only a few minutes, Cheryl's makeup began to run and blisters started forming on her toes. She wasn't a very happy hiker and became more and more upset and downright pissed off that we had even thought of this "crater experience" in the first place.

Gale, of course, had on his Nike's and was practically jumping for joy the whole way. I didn't think it was so bad, but I was getting concerned about Cheryl. We had hit the hot zone, and she was getting madder by the minute. Her makeup had already sweated off, and her snow-white skin was getting sunburned. It seemed like at least 100 degrees.

We had begun to shed much of the clothing we had on, just left them where they dropped. We had no water, no food, nothing.

The only way to get to the other side of the crater was through an endless series of switchbacks, and when it looked like you were almost there, you were just beginning. Cheryl's face, each time I passed her, changed. She literally looked like she wanted to kill someone. She could barely walk, and I really felt for her. But we all were hurting by this time. We finally made our way out of the crater just before dark, and Cheryl didn't talk to me for several days afterward.

I tried to make it up to her, and she finally came around. But we had to go to Honolulu for a meeting with the Outdoor Circle, which she wasn't too happy about; this was supposed to be her vacation. Nonetheless, she agreed to go and support me. We were carrying several portfolios each, full of artwork, pictures and slides. We both had as much as we could carry. Our Korean cabby didn't speak any English and, even though we told him the correct address, he still dropped us off about 15 blocks — long blocks — from the Outdoor Circle's office in Honolulu. He sped away as soon as we got out of the car.

Again, the heat was unbearable, and we were both melting, irritable and mad. We went into the nearest building and were told it was the wrong one, that the building we were looking for was 15 blocks away. I was already 15 minutes late, and there were no other cabs in sight.

"Look, we gotta walk," I informed her.

"I'm not walking," she fired back.

Then, after a moment's hesitation, she threw all of my bags on the hot pavement and stormed away. She just stomped out of there, leaving me with twice as many bags as I had before. The 15 hot blocks were like a marathon as I struggled and dragged the portfolios and bags the entire way. I arrived at the Outdoor Circle's door completely stressed out and drenched with sweat.

"You're late," said the hard-faced elderly woman who opened the door.

"I'm really sorry; we had a hard time with our cab driver," I said, trying to catch my breath.

"I don't care," she snorted. "Our time is very important here."

"Well, I'm really sorry, but I would like to explain this

mural I'm going to be painting," I said.

"Wait a minute, wait a minute, you're not painting any mural anywhere," she said regally, as if God himself had put her in charge. "This is Hawaii, and we don't allow murals."

This rude woman was none other than Betty Crocker, whose name was the misnomer of the century. A far cry from the sweet country-kitchen mother we all associate with baking products, she reminded me of the wicked witch in *The Wizard of Oz*.

"If only you would allow me to show you some of my work," I pleaded politely. Her lips, which I'm not sure were ever there in the first place, seemed to tighten, and her eyes narrowed. Winning the Outdoor Circle over was looking very unrealistic at this moment. One of the ladies standing nearby, however, was sympathetic and invited me in. We sat down quickly and started to open my portfolio when Betty Crocker reached over and closed it with one of her claws.

"We don't need to see it," she said.

A tense moment took forever to pass. I was starting to wonder why I had even bothered to meet these people. Finally, I cleared my throat and tried one last time: "You know, I really didn't have to come to this meeting. The mural has already been approved by the city and neighborhood board. I just wanted to come by and share what I do with you."

Betty Crocker sat back in her throne, surrounded by her three sub-members. The ugly look on her face told me the whole story. The others, I could tell, were curious about the project, but the group had already made up its mind, or had it made up for them. There was just no way they were going to let this happen.

It was a very short, negative meeting during which they told me the mural was an advertising billboard. They didn't appear to hear or understand a word I was saying when I told them: "No, this is a mural that is going to depict Hawaii's state marine mammal, the humpback whale, and the other marine life and beauty that is native to Hawaiian waters. This mural is very important."

Slowly, I got up to leave. As I was zipping my portfolio, Betty Crocker put her curse on me: "You will never paint this wall in Honolulu," she hissed, her voice dripping with venom that came from who the hell knows where.

"I already have. . . I already painted it up here in my

mind's eye," I said, pointing to my brain. "It's going to be beautiful. Come by and see it."

The lady who had let me into the Circle's den, walked out with me and offered me a ride back to the Outrigger Reef Hotel in Waikiki, which I gratefully accepted. I left my luggage in my room and left again to see if I could buy some concert tickets for that evening. Dan Fogelberg, who would later become a good friend of mine, was doing a concert that night at the Waikiki Shell, and I thought this might be a great way to score some points with Cheryl so she might forget how mad she was.

I gave the lady at the ticket office the whole mad-girl-friend story, and she gave me front-row tickets for that night. I raced back to the hotel and into the room, where there was a note on the bed that read: "F.O." It was basically a f - - - off and die "Dear John" note. You know — you're the biggest asshole in the world; you ruined my vacation; you work too much. I admit to being a workaholic, and this wall was very important to me. But I really cared about this girl. I took it real hard; it was terrible and I was very sad. I went ahead to the concert that night, but Dan Fogelberg's sad, sad songs from the heart made it very hard to listen. It was a beautiful tropical night, and I kept wishing she were there. But she had boarded a plane and gone back to Canada. I later told Dan Fogelberg the whole story, and we both had a good laugh. But it wasn't funny at the time.

The next month, the pressure and rhetoric from the Outdoor Circle started to heat up so I decided it was time to get going on the mural. The word on the street was that the Circle was going to come down heavy on this project. I thought if I could get the mural painted over the holidays I would have a pretty good chance of getting it up. My other strategy was to paint such a beautiful mural that the people would come to my rescue.

It was Christmas Eve, and we worked all day getting the scaffolding and stages set up. I wanted to start real early on Christmas Day because I was very concerned about overspray. When you're using large, airless spray guns, you have to be concerned about getting paint on cars. My crew and I — six of us — were staying in a single donated room at the Waikikian Hotel. It was cramped, but the price was right. We got our wake-up call and went down to the wall at 3 a.m. to start spraying. We figured this mural was going to require 3,000 gallons of paint. It was by far the largest mural I had ever undertaken, and one of the largest murals in the world.

As we walked up to the wall, we were shocked to find a dead body lying in a heap beneath the scaffolding. It was Christmas morning, and I understand there are a lot of suicides during the holidays. We later learned that this poor soul had been a doctor who had jumped the 20 stories to his death, right in front of the mural. To me, it was a sign — an omen — and not a good one. Anyone who knows me knows I am terrified of heights, and my biggest fear was to have to go up there and paint that tower. But I had to do it right then because I needed to get it out of the way. The higher you go, the more chance there is of overspray, and I didn't want any cars around.

After we got over the initial shock of watching the body being scraped off the cement, literally, the cops and ambulance came. It was weighing heavy on my mind because I was preparing to go up the same 20 stories and paint. We mixed the paint, hooked the airless gun to the scaffolding and were ready to go up and start at the top. I had a death-grip (sorry) on the scaffold as we rode the motors up. At about the 18th story, we suddenly had a power surge. One of the motors snaffued, and a cable line broke right in half, sending an electrical cable with a short dangling near me. All of a sudden, the scaffold dropped about six feet. There I was thinking about that dead body, and it was almost totally dark outside. Then this thing drops six feet when I'm 18 stories in the air! The only thing below me was the parking lot. I mean. . . I saw God.

I had three choices: hang on, repel down the wall or call the fire department. I chose to hang on for my life. What kept going through my mind was the guy who had just jumped. That was definitely not the way I wanted to be remembered — a martyr. Eventually, one of our guys repelled down the wall and fixed the cable. It had been a real life and death situation. I was so thankful when they got the motor fixed and brought me down. I had to sit on the ground for awhile to get myself back together. I was shaking so badly I could hardly stand up.

Of course, I had to get back up there. I had to get on the scaffold and go back up the 20 stories and start spraying. Once I did start spraying, everything felt better. Plus, the sun had come up. But the calm was short-lived. I had the sprayer going full-blast when all of a sudden the wind kicked up and carried a large cloud of blue paint across the Ala Wai and over the tops of 70 boats and 90 cars within a half-mile radius. I watched in horror as I painted all of these vessels and vehicles my own shade of blue. There was no way I could deny it. This was Wyland blue! It had been a bizarre morning. I had a million dollars worth of insurance that covered overspray, so I just kept on painting.

As it got lighter outside, I could see people showing up below me. They were looking at the blue paint on their cars and definitely pointing their fingers at me. I told them it would wash right off. As soon as I could get to a phone, I called Sinclair Paint and asked how to get the paint off of these cars. Sinclair told me it was two-part epoxy sealer, the best and most durable paint in the world. They informed me it would take a chisel to get it off of a car.

A chisel! My Adam's Apple just dropped. Boy, was I in big trouble. I especially knew I was in trouble when a group of Samoans asked me to come down and talk to them about their blue-speckled cars. Still high on the scaffold, I decided it was time to take a lunch break. I took the scaffold up to the roof, went out the back door and left for the rest of the day, hoping nobody would notice.

Judge Saves Wyland's Whaling Wall

My insurance guy showed up the next day and explained to me that I had painted 70 boats and 90 cars and no longer had any insurance. They had canceled it on the spot when they were barraged by so many inquiries. They had to spend the entire million to repaint everything. I had to finish the Honolulu Whaling Wall with no insurance.

The tower's background had been completed, however, and I felt pretty good about moving forward on the mural, which I did at a very fast pace. I completed the background work by the first week and was preparing the paint for the first whale. When I did finish the first whale, a guy came over from Kaiser Hospital very excited. He said his wife was in the hospital having a baby at that very moment, and they had been watching me paint from their hospital room. I went up and painted a baby whale in their honor. He came back out and told me how fantastic and symbolic it was to have his baby born at the same time. It was very touching, gave me goosebumps.

Everything progressed rather nicely for a few days after that. I had several whales swimming across a 300-foot blue ocean when I heard these shrill voices below me. At first, I didn't pay much attention. There were at least 100 people on the ground watching me and making plenty of noise. But then I realized that these voices were rising above the sounds from the rest of the crowd and being directed at me. I looked down and saw a small group, mostly old ladies, standing there with rollers and what looked to be cans of paint.

"WE'RE GOING TO STOP YOU. . ." one of the ladies squawked at me. "WE'RE GOING TO PAINT THIS WALL WHITE. WE'RE GOING TO STOP YOU."

I came down off the scaffold and talked to Marge McDowell, who was part of the normal audience of onlookers. She told me these were Outdoor Circle people and that they had, indeed, gotten a court injunction and that I was about to be sued and dragged into court for painting a public mural. She told me the Circle had plotted with a big developer named Jack Meyers, as well as the Waikiki Improvement Association, to sign a petition to get a court order to stop me from painting the wall, and to paint it out before it was even finished.

What was really happening was that Meyers had purchased the property under Kaiser Hospital next door and was planning to tear the hospital down and build a luxury hotel in its place. The growing public support for the mural was posing a threat to his hotel because it was designed such that it would cover most of the mural. It was Meyers' attorneys and money that were being used to take the mural to court and stop it before it garnered any more attention. He had his agenda, and he was exactly the resource the Outdoor Circle needed. These were all contentious people who were more than skillful than I at doing whatever it took to meet their needs.

As for me, I knew I had a battle on my hands. But I believed in what I was doing and figured that the response to this Whaling Wall was going to be so sensational that the public would step in and make sure that good won out over evil. The crows from the Outdoor Circle stood around beneath the mural for a while that morning, I guess. I ignored them and returned to my wall and my whales. I think they were sort of quieted and intimidated by the rest of the crowd, which was growing by the hour.

When I appeared in court a few days later, though, my concentration as an artist was replaced by the worry and fear of losing my work. I was very nervous. Meyers and the Outdoor Circle had two or three attorneys present, and there was media everywhere. This fabricated controversy had suddenly grown from a local story to a national and even international story. AP and UPI picked it up; it was all over the place. I had been working on the mural for about three weeks and was half-done. But I was starting to really get scared it would be painted over before I was finished.

They made a good run at it. With Meyers and Betty Crocker sitting smugly behind them, their attorneys claimed the mural was disgusting, an "eyesore" the public should not have to look at and that it was actually a billboard. Then they started in on me: "He's not even from Hawaii. What does he care about our. . ." They basically used every lame argument they could think of — full attack.

I had never been through anything like this in my life. It was a real eye-opener to watch such a blatant distortion of reality receive enough credibility to even be presented in a court of law. Fortunately, the Ilikai Homeowners, who were furious about the attempt to stop the mural, and even more furious about being named as a co-defendant in the lawsuit, had hired attorney Reid Nakamura to represent them. I certainly had no money but, for the sum of one painting, Reid also represented me.

Judge Saves Wyland's Whaling Wall

In his closing remarks, Reid hit what I thought was the telling blow for State Judge Philip Chun. "Here is this guy who wants to give a gift to the State of Hawaii and wants to raise the consciousness of people about whales and our marine life. And what do we give him back? We give him COURT!"

Judge Chun wasted no time in his ruling. He told the court and, thanks to the media, the world that he himself had been by the mural and that it was, indeed, a work of art and not a sign or a billboard. He said his kids were with him and couldn't stop talking about it. In fact, he said, everyone he had talked to liked it and thought it was a good thing for the state.

I won't pretend to know what else the judge might have considered in rendering his opinion, and I don't want to cast any kind of shadow on his objectivity. But he would have had to be blind not to recognize the real motives behind what Meyers and the Outdoor Circle were doing. He wasn't buying any of it. He stood up and proclaimed the mural was not a sign or billboard, that it was a work of public art and that he was in favor of it staying where it was. The headlines the next morning in *The Honolulu Advertiser* read:

"JUDGE SAVES WYLAND'S WHALING WALL."

It was the greatest victory I had ever had. In my exuberance, I didn't even think about looking back at Jack Meyers or Betty Crocker in triumph. Besides, I'm not sure I would have wanted to see Betty's face turn any meaner than it already was.

"Don't say anything," my attorney said as we approached the awaiting media outside the courtroom.

"Are you kidding?" I said, incredulously. "I've been waiting a long time to share this story."

The media was very positive and supportive. It was a tremendous victory not only for the plight of public art in the State of Hawaii, but also for the whales. I truly believe it wasn't only the judge who saved the wall, but it was the people — the spirit of the people of Hawaii. They had rallied to protect it because they felt it represented an important part of Hawaii's maritime history. Later on, the Whaling Wall would become one of the favorite landmarks in the state. In fact, Kodak wrote me a letter stating it was the second most photographed landmark in Hawaii, second only to Diamond Head.

The following day I was back on the wall painting. The

newspaper carried a political cartoon of me on the scaffolding with little angels flying around me. It was just great, people driving by and beeping their horns and saying hello to me. The Whaling Wall was in the media nonstop for four months afterward, mostly letters to the editor and editorials supporting it. Meyers and the Outdoor Circle had to pay all of my attorney fees, which I'm sure added insult to their perceived injury. I was told they wanted to get even really badly. There were even threats flying around that I would never live to finish the wall. Each day afterward I had to check the scaffolding and make sure the hooks were secure and the bolts were tight before I painted.

We finished the wall on Earth Day, April 22, 1985, literally two hours before the dedication. It was a very special ceremony. A Hawaiian priest blessed the wall, and a plaque was installed identifying the whales and marine life I had depicted in the painting. Russ Francis, the professional football player and one of Hawaii's favorite sons, dedicated the wall. It was a glorious moment. Each day after the dedication, the wall drew more and more people. I was invited by the Japanese to do a wall in Japan after they saw it. It was one of the main launching pads for my career.

Without knowing it, the Outdoor Circle had provided more media for the project than any public relations firm could have. I would like to thank them for that.

I later received a proclamation from the Hawaii State Senate for the mural. Ironically, on the same day they presented it to me, the Outdoor Circle was receiving a proclamation for planting trees. Betty Crocker, the grande dame, was there to receive the award, and she "stink-eyed" me the whole time. Maybe she thought she could reactivate the failed curse she had placed on me that day in her office, I don't know. I do know, however, that she has yet to give up on trashing my character. *Honolulu Magazine*, whose present publisher is a member of the Outdoor Circle, printed a feature article on Betty Crocker several years later in which she lied through her teeth. She said that on our first meeting I had come into her office and put my feet on her desk and that I was very brash young man. I never did any of that. It was totally untrue. I had been as polite as I could be. I try to be polite to older people because I know I'm going to have to be one someday.

The epilogue to this story is interesting, at least to me it is. Before he sold it to a Japanese investor, Jack Meyers, the developer, built his luxury hotel, the Hawaii Prince, so that it obscured most of the wall and destroyed the mural. I feel, in a way, like this was a symbol for what is happening to the environment. That a developer would go ahead and build with no respect for what was already there is an appropriate metaphor for what has been happening to the whales on this planet — they are being closed out by man.

But the mural is still doing what it was supposed to do — raise consciousness. Everyone who drives by the hotel and remembers the Whaling Wall, and there are a lot of repeat visitors to Hawaii, can see that a developer destroyed a beautiful piece of art. Even today, I continue to hear people express their disgust over what became of the mural.

I was told that a lot of Outdoor Circle members quit because of the whole debacle. Several members actually contacted me and apologized. They came up to me and said they were embarrassed by Betty Crocker and the stance she took. In fact, the day we were in court, State Senator Neil Abercrombie, who now is a U.S. Congressman from Hawaii, came up to me and said, "Wyland, what you're doing is very valuable and important in the State of Hawaii. I'm embarrassed by the Outdoor Circle and by their view of murals."

Abercrombie told me he would do anything he could to try and change some of the laws so an artist would have the right to protect his work. He then marched into Judge Chun's quarters and told him that for the Outdoor Circle to even impact this mural at all was ridiculous and frivolous. In my opinion, the Outdoor Circle has done a good job keeping billboards out of Hawaii, and I support their work on that. They've also planted a lot of trees in the state. But they were dead wrong on this particular issue, and I think a lot of their members knew that. I think they need to rethink how they view murals, instead of just saying they are all bad and don't belong in Hawaii.

This one sure belonged where it was, and it is missed by many people. Maybe its demise will help open the door for other murals to be painted in Hawaii in the future. The Honolulu Whaling Wall was a wonderful example of how murals can enrich our lives, even if we only get to see them for a little while.

Judge Saves Wyland's Whaling Wall

6

Painting Whales in Japan

*...We have much to learn from the whales, they are much more
valuable to us alive...we must save them...*

WYLAND

*B*y 1987, the Whaling Wall in Honolulu had become one of the most visible murals in the world. I was particularly happy that so many Japanese tourists who had visited Hawaii were exposed to the painting and, as a result, to the magnificence of lifesize whales in their habitat.

Ironically, it was the president of the Tokyo Bay Fishing Association, Mr. Ono, who contacted a good friend of mine from the *Hawaii Ho Chi* newspaper, Tamaki Sarbaugh. I had known Tamaki for a few years; she had been covering my work in the islands. She approached me about a Mr. Ono, who had inquired about me flying to Japan to paint a Whaling Wall there. I had, for some time, really wanted to do this because Japan is one of the last countries in the world still involved in commercial whaling. I thought it would be an important work of art, but I was having a lot of anxieties about it. I wasn't sure how I would be received the culture was so entirely different. But I decided it was necessary to make the trip.

Mr. Ono insisted on flying Tamaki and me to Funabashi. He had found a perfect wall, a seawall right on Tokyo Bay. The concern was that the Tokyo shoreline was being developed at an alarming rate, killing off the entire ecosystem in the shallows and impacting all of its fish and marine life. Mr. Ono and his association were very concerned and felt that if I could come and paint a Whaling Wall there, it would draw attention to their issue. It was kind of strange, actually, a Japanese fisherman, the president of a fishing association, asking me to paint a Whaling Wall. Nonetheless, off we went to Japan. Tamaki and I spent the entire 11-hour flight talking about Japanese culture, which is much more formal and intricate than I could ever have imagined. Tamaki, born and raised in Tokyo, was trying to teach me the Japanese ways. She was very excited because she was going to visit her parents in Tokyo, whom she hadn't seen for many years.

For me, I was wondering what kind of reaction the wall

would get from Japanese citizens. This could be a really big deal, I thought. It might be the first time many Japanese would see a whale, other than on their dinner plate. I was being given a tremendous opportunity to make a statement that could be heard around the country, and around the world.

We were greeted at the airport by Mr. Ono himself. He was very short and stocky, a strong, middle-aged Japanese man. He was a handsome fellow, called by his friends the "Robert Redford of Japan." His warm, smiling face belied a vice-like handshake that almost crushed my hand. He was definitely a fisherman. I later discovered he was a fisherman from a long line of fishermen.

He insisted that we stay at his home, which was a very large, traditional Japanese house in a town called Chiba, just outside of Tokyo. The tradition when guests were arriving was to have a welcoming party. When we entered the front door, we were greeted by 40 people, all, like Mr. Ono, with warm smiles on their faces. It was traditional to meet every-one in the family upon arriving, so we removed our shoes and met not only Mr. Ono's family, but everyone, including the City Council members and people from the Tokyo Bay

Fishing Association, who were involved in the project. It was an overwhelming greeting that carried on late into the evening, with an entire feast of varying Japanese cuisine and beer. Lots of beer. When you leave, they have a sayanara party, and the same people who had gathered to greet you were present to say good-bye.

At the welcoming party, though, I remember being impressed that so many people had turned out to greet us and that they appeared to be so committed to helping me out with the project. It truly was to be a pioneering effort. No American has ever gone to Japan and painted a mural with such political significance. It was ironic that back in the States I was pretty much a starving artist during this period. But in Japan, this was big news. A writer from the Japan Times was at the party working on a cover story. I was told that evening that they had everything lined up, and the story had already broken there. They had selected the wall, which already had some small murals on it that children throughout Japan had painted. The kids' wall stretched almost a mile long, but they had saved the tallest section for me.

The customs of the Ono's household were a bit of a shock to me, to say the least. We slept on futons on the floor and, of course, had to take the baths at night — the traditional baths. First you'd take a shower and then go into the bath, where you sat on a little stool. The toilet situation was different, too. You had to squat over a little hole, where I lost my wallet several times during my stay. I finally started carrying it in my front pocket so I wouldn't forget. There's no dignity in going down there to get your wallet!

The food, although quite delicious, was also different than what I was used to. Number one, my hosts were gracious enough to let me sleep but, at 3:00 every morning, Mr. Ono, his father and his sons would head out to their fishing vessels to fish for sardines in Tokyo Bay. By the time I got out of bed — about 8:00 or 9:00 — they were already back and eating. In fact, they were usually finished and just waiting for me to arrive. When I did finally mosey on downstairs to the kitchen area, I ate the traditional Japanese breakfast, which is fish and more fish, and beer. Yes, beer for breakfast; Kam-pai, first thing in the morning. This was totally unique for me because I don't even drink. But, to be sociable, I got used to drinking beer first thing in the morning . . . for lunch. . . and so on.

After breakfast we went down to the wall site, and I

looked out on Tokyo Bay. The first thing I noticed was a fleet of deadly looking whaling vessels with their harpoons standing sentry over their bows. Everything I had ever read about and seen on film about whalers was right in front of me. It was perfect! I was thrilled to be standing there to see first-hand a real whaling village and, in fact, a whaling culture. I decided to paint sperm whales because the wall looked large enough, and because the animals had been hunted by the Japanese for hundreds of years for their oil and other products.

The Japanese company that had donated all the paint and spray guns had everything ready for us. The Japanese are a very generous people and are used to paying for everything. I had a hard time convincing them the mural was free, that I was donating my time to do it. Finally, I had to alter my story a bit and tell them it was to be a gift to their country, appealing to their fierce nationalism. This was totally unallowed in their country, they told me. But finally they relented. Through my interpreter, one of the men said, "Free costs more." I found out later he was right.

When we started on the background, there was a lot of excitement and curiosity. Their curiosity grew as I painted the first whale, called Kujira, and then another named Cachalot. By the time I had finished the first sperm whale, traffic had stopped on the streets. People came by the thousands to stop and take pictures. Being an American painting a lifesize living whale in Japan was, to say the least, quite an oddity that created much discussion below me. Although I didn't understand the language, I sensed they were talking about the attention the wall would bring to the area.

We were supposed to be there 10 days, but I finished the wall in three. The sudden transformation of the wall had begun to draw national attention, particularly from the press. One night, through Mr. Ono, I met one of the editors of Japan's largest newspaper, the *Asahi Simbu*. He had come to cover the mural, and we were scheduled to meet for dinner at Mr. Ono's seafood restaurant, a cozy little establishment in Tokyo with only five or six tables. We took the subway train to get there and, when we arrived, found 15 guests awaiting us at one of the tables. It seemed at first that everyone was a little nervous being in the company of an editor from the country's largest paper, a man who wielded a lot of power. But, as the beer and sake started lining the tops of the tables, things loosened up in a hurry. They did bring out some food, but it was largely neglected. These guys had definitely shown up that evening to drink. And drink they did.

The newspaper man spoke very little English, which didn't matter after a while. And I guess he decided at one point to liven up the party by ordering some gin. Two bottles were rushed out to the table, and he poured two drinks over ice and handed one of them to me. I looked at the straight gin and decided I couldn't say no; I had to participate in this cultural thing. So I drank a couple of drinks with him and decided to play the game by ordering four more bottles of gin for everyone. I didn't have to speak the language. I just held up four fingers, and a waiter quickly brought the bottles to the table. I then opened all of them and emptied them into a gallon-size ice container from which I started chugging. I suppose I was getting a little beyond cultural at this point but, what the hell, Americans have always done things in a big way. After three or four chugs, I handed the ice bucket to the editor, who, in my fuzzy estimation, was way past the point of no return, way past. But I wanted to make this a memorable evening so I started chanting, "Go. . . go. . . go."

In this kind of loosely officiated game, it's okay if you take three or four chugs and quit. But this guy just kept on going. All of the guests in the restaurant were pounding on the table and chanting with me, "Go. . . go. . . go. . . go. . ." I'm not sure if he was all that familiar with chugging contests, but he won hands-down. In victory, he leaned back in his chair and tipped it over backwards, landing on the floor like a 100-pound sack of rice. There he lay, passed out with his arms and legs sprawled to either side with ice and gin spilled all over him. Everyone in the room stood up and gave him a standing ovation, after which some little guy came out of the kitchen and mopped him down like he was a piece of linoleum.

We couldn't wake the guy up so several of our comrades picked him up, stripped him down to his underwear and laid him right in the middle of our table. It must have been 2:30 in the morning, and many in the room were but two shades shy of being stripped and placed on one of the tables themselves. They really got crazy at that point, placing fish and different kinds of sushi all over the good editor's body and head. A big tuna suddenly appeared, breaching out of his BVD's, and they started taking pictures of him. It was wild and perversely funny, I guess. I felt a little sorry for him when they started using him as a table, though. Men and women were placing their glasses and beer bottles on him like he was an extension of the liquor-soaked table. At least he was no longer part of the floor. Later, when Mr. Ono was ready to lock up for the night and the editor couldn't be aroused, they threw a tablecloth over him and left him where he lay, sushi-adorned and at peace with the world. I kept wondering what he was going to think the next morning when he came to and found that tuna in his shorts.

Everything was spinning for me as we left the restaurant, but the evening was far from over. We went out to sing karaoke after that, more beers, more of everything, when all of a sudden they wanted to go fishing. I was horrified. Me, Captain Chum, with a belly full of alcohol and raw fish. I had seen how rough Tokyo Bay was, the small boats rocking back and forth on its surface. I wasn't gonna to do no chumming with no Japanese with cameras. After much debate, Tamaki came to my rescue and took me home in a cab. A few days later I would run into the esteemed editor. "So solly, Mr. Wyland, so solly," he said profusely. I guess I'd be a little humbled myself if I had awakened in his condition. But he wrote a very flattering article about the whole evening with me. It was nothing at all like what really happened, of course, which was just as well for both of us. Evidently, reporters in Japan, just like in America, know how to take care of themselves. I have no complaints; with a few exceptions, the press in both countries have taken pretty good care of me.

The next morning was one big hangover for me. Mr. Ono and his sons had been out fishing and were already at the breakfast table drinking beer when I finally made it out of my room. His entire family just smiled, nodded their heads and said "No problem" when I pointed to my head to describe my headache. "O hyo gonzios kam pai," they said, which means "Yeah, have another beer and bite the dog that killed the chicken," or something like that. As I raised my glass, the whole family chanted, "Go. . . Go. . . Go. . ."

Later that day, Mr. Ono received a call from the mayor of Taiji inquiring as to whether I might be interested in visiting his fair town. Thanks to the press coverage on the Funabashi wall, the mayor had evidently learned of the mural. He didn't want me to come and paint a Whaling Wall;

he just wanted me to visit. I had heard and studied about Taiji, where whaling had started in Japan over 400 years ago. Mr. Ono told me the town had become a tourist destination with a museum that had all the old whaling artifacts. Naturally, I wanted to go. I considered this to be research that could become a very important aspect of my work. Taiji was one of the last places in the world that was still involved in coastal whaling.

It took about eight hours to make the journey, six hours by bullet train, two by subway, and then a short boat ride out to the island. I was traveling with Tamaki, Lorne Green, a photographer friend of mine from Canada, and Kevin Short, a feature writer with the *Japan Times* who had lived in Japan for some time and was covering my visit to the country. We were greeted at the train station by Mr. Kyoto, Taiji's City Manager, who quickly explained to us that my trip to Taiji was very important because the township wanted to share their side of the whaling issue with me. Artists are highly respected in Japan, and they felt my visit would help promote Taiji, which had come under attack from the rest of the world for its continued hunting of whales.

Painting Whales in Japan

Before taking us to the mayor's office, Mr. Kyoto drove us around the town. We went by the whaling museum, a huge building that had a giant tile mosaic of an abstract right whale near its entrance. The first thing I noticed was a huge blank wall on the side front entrance to the museum — very visible, hmmm. . .

"This is a perfect wall for a mural," I told Mr. Kyoto, as we both looked at the side of the museum. "I would love to come back to Taiji one day and paint a Whaling Wall right here. Wouldn't that be nice?"

"Yes, Mr. Wyland, that would be very beautiful," he replied with a grin on his face.

As we neared City Hall, it struck me that everything in this town revolved around whales. Their town symbol was a whale. The signs, everything was whales! Over 80 percent of the population in Taiji was involved somehow in whaling. This was a true whaling village and, yes, they still killed whales. But, in their own way, they honored and respected them as well. It had been part of their culture since 1606, when they killed the first great whale, Semi Kujira, or right whale. They were called right whales because they were the right whales to kill — unlike other large whales, they didn't sink after being harpooned.

We met with the mayor and all the city officials, who were very gracious. We drank green tea and talked for hours through Tamaki about whaling. They said they just wanted to preserve their whaling heritage, and that it seemed as if the whole world was against them and thought they were bad people. The mayor told me they wanted me to see that they were, in reality, a good people and that they honored the whale. This, they hoped, would help me, as a visible artist, to be more neutral.

They said they hadn't caught many whales of late and, in fact, hadn't even seen any for a long while. I told them that where I lived in Hawaii there were so many whales off the shores that whale watching had become very successful. I acknowledged that Americans had, at one time, been involved in Yankee whaling, but I informed them that whale watching had replaced whaling as an industry, not only in the United States, but throughout the world. I didn't want to be too pushy, but I suggested to them that if they should stop whaling and start whale watching, they had a unique opportunity to bolster their visitor industry like other cities had done — cities like Lahaina, San Diego and Boston, to name a few. The mayor and his colleagues nodded that they understood what I was talking about and, in fact, had already taken it into consideration. However, they explained, it was critical to them that they preserve their 400 years of whaling history, and they wanted to continue to kill whales.

As I absorbed this information, I told them I was simply trying through my art to teach people about the living whales so they would know and understand them better. It's important to note that the people of Taiji were whale fanatics, like me. They knew every type of whale in the sea and every detail about each of them. The only problem was that most of their knowledge was from hunting whales, and most of the whales they had seen were dead. My knowledge, on the other hand, was derived from living whales. My mind kept racing back to the museum wall, and I recognized that this could be an opportunity to bridge the gap. The mayor and I were getting along quite well and, as I was leaving, I presented him with some of my prints, and he had some gifts for me. He invited me to come back to Taiji anytime, and there was my chance.

"Thank you very much," I said. "I would like to come back and paint one of my Whaling Walls here. I saw a really nice blank wall on the side of the museum. If you could get permission, I would love to come over and paint it."

The mayor's face slowly transformed into a big smile, and he said, "Perhaps one day." I had planted a seed. Several years later, I would receive an invitation from the new mayor of Taiji to come back and paint the wall, which I did.

We walked out of City Hall into a bright sunny day. Taiji is a beautiful little city, a resort area very unlike Tokyo; the water is blue and clear, like in Hawaii, with gorgeous, lush green mountains and hot springs. As my eyes ventured out into the bay, I couldn't believe what I saw next. An entire pod of whales were being herded by 15 to 18 fishing boats, right there in front of City Hall! I couldn't tell from that distance what kind they were, but could see they were relatively small. I asked the mayor if I could go down and observe what was happening. He said yes, and we all walked down to the water and watched as the Japanese boats strictly herded the whales into a little lagoon. When the last whale had entered, a net came across the mouth of the lagoon and trapped them. Talk about timing and fate, I had read about this in history books, but watching it happen right in front of me was like a mirage. It was incredible. I was just leaving an important conversation in the mayor's office about these creatures, and I was scheduled to leave the next day. I never, in my wildest dreams, expected to see something like this.

That night, at the Right Whale Hotel, I couldn't sleep thinking about the real, captured whales. At 4 a.m., I couldn't take it anymore. So I woke Kevin and Lorne up and said I was going to go take a look. They, of course, were there to cover me and my visit, so they begrudgingly got up and hiked down to the water behind me. When I say "hiked," that's exactly what we had to do — over mountains and hills. It took some walking to get down to the lagoon. It was still dark, but the moonlight helped me identify the whales right off as being short-fin pilot whales. There were about 30 adults in the group, all protecting a big male with a bulbous head. I had seen these whales at Sea World in California and in Hawaii, but this male was the biggest short-fin pilot whale I had ever seen.

Then I saw two babies popping up beside their mothers, and I almost lost it. "What a shame," I thought. With this type of whaling occurring, an entire family — no, an entire generation — is killed off at once, with no chance of recovery. While they might not kill the babies, they would die anyway without their mother to take care of them. It's not like they were going to just take some of the bigger whales, and the others could go on and reproduce. No, these whales were all together so they could be slaughtered right there in the bay and sold as fish.

The whales saw us standing near the edge of the water and moved away a little. The two babies made me very sentimental and I thought, "Jesus! This is terrible. What's going to happen here?" I became frantic, trying to think what to do, when, for some reason I can't explain, I got down to my BVD's and dove into the cold, dark water. And when I say cold, I mean COLD. But it didn't matter to me. At least it was warmer than Tokyo Bay, where I had tried to swim earlier in the week. Actually, the sun was starting to come up, and the lagoon was taking on colors and light that made it quite beautiful. Teeth chattering, I swam over to the whales and, after a few minutes, they started moving toward me as a group to check me out. My friends on shore were telling each other I was absolutely crazy, but Lorne soon started taking some pictures.

Although these were large animals being held against

their will, I wasn't afraid or anything. To me, I was simply swimming in a lagoon with some friends. I swam over them, treading water, when I noticed what looked to be a scout whale swimming below me back and forth along the net. Then I saw the babies again. I decided I had to do something. People talk about saving whales, and I didn't want to be radical or anything, but I just couldn't stand by and watch the babies be killed! I started thinking about a way to let them go, some way of letting the net go. I swam over to the scout and saw that the net was tied off on a tree at the inlet. Before I could act further, however, my friend Kevin had figured out what I was thinking and had stripped down to his BVD's and jumped in the water with me.

"Don't do it, Wyland!" he yelled at me across the surface. He was not a pretty site — red hair, freckles and flabby, fish-belly white skin. He looked so unnatural out in the water with these whales. Then again, I guess I did, too. "I know what you want to do, but don't do it," he said. "You've painted a mural, and the Japanese people are starting to respect you. If you let these whales go, all of your efforts it will go out the window.

"Besides, these whalers are not going to take too kindly

to your letting these whales go," he continued. "They've been waiting a long time for them. Look! Here they come now."

Sure enough, eight small boats were heading our way from a distance to "process" the whales. "Your thoughts are good, Wyland, but you're going to make a much bigger impact on the Japanese people if you come back and paint a mural," Kevin pleaded.

I was reaching a crisis point. My conscience wouldn't let me leave these wonderful creatures behind to be killed, but to do anything to interfere would have been disastrous. Kevin was right. Saving 32 whales from sure death would have been right as well. But the whalers would just find another 32, and then 32 more after that. I could come back and paint more murals in Japan and perhaps affect the country's entire whaling industry. This would save many more whales in the long run.

After what I'm sure seemed like eternity to Kevin and Lorne, I relented, and we swam back to shore just before the whalers reached the lagoon. They weren't looking for two Americans in the water, anyway. They had whaling on their minds. Soaking wet, we hiked back to the hotel. This was one of the lowest points in my life. Whales were my subjects as an artist, and I felt a responsibility to protect them. My work was dedicated to helping man learn about and appreciate them so they could be saved from extinction. This experience made me even more determined to continue through public art to create awareness around the world that whales are worthy of protection.

Word got out that morning that I had swum with these whales, and the Taiji township wouldn't let me out of their sight until I left that afternoon. They escorted us to the train station and put someone on the train to make sure we left.

To this day, I haven't completely gotten over this whole episode. It was the hardest decision I ever made and, even though I later received a lot of hate mail from certain environmentalists when word about it spread, I think it was the right decision. I truly believe that if I had released these whales, it would have had a negative effect on the Japanese people and destroyed the trust and respect my art had gained.

I have now painted four Whaling Walls in Japan, including the most important one in Taiji. The mayor I had met with that day died shortly afterward, and the new mayor eventually invited me to Taiji to paint a mural. I painted a lifesize right whale and her calf on the wall I had seen on the side of the whaling museum. The Japanese have now begun whale watching for the first time in their history, shooting them with cameras instead of harpoons. I will be returning in the winter of 1995 on my Asia Whaling Wall Tour to paint even more murals in this beautiful country. My work in Japan will forever be dedicated to my 32 friends who perished that morning in the lagoon by Taiji.

Painting Whales in Japan

Whale Tales

nother day at Laguna Beach

photo by Greg O'Loughin

◄ With olde
brother S
(me on le

▲ Our house in Madison Heights, Michigan

◄ Me, Bill and Steve

▲ Lamphere varsity basketball team #44
◀ Painting in studio
◀ My airbrush teacher Dennis Poosch,
   (Shrunken Head Studios)
▲ Varsity football, Lamphere Rams

▲ At first Whaling Wall in Laguna Beach, California

photo by Bob T

Mom and me at our annual Wyland Galleries Show

▲ Family; Tom, Steve, Bill, Mom and me at my home on the North Shore of Oahu

▲ Sunset at Laguna Beach, California

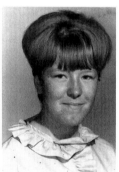

▲Friend, Tom Klingenmeier   ▲ Aunt Terri Sell   ▲ Early above and below painting - 1971

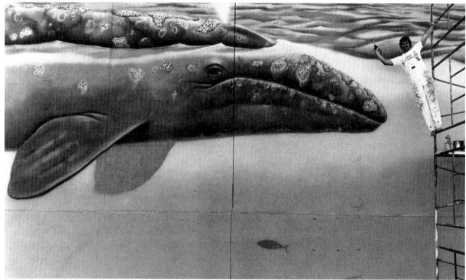

▲ Finishing lifesize Gray Whale, Whaling Wall 1, Laguna Beach - 1981

▲ Whaling Wall 1, Laguna Beach, California - 1981

▲ Swimming with Atlantic Bottlenose Dolphin, Florida

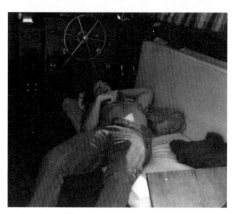

▲ Captain Chum

▲ Me, Bird Baker, J.D. Mahew, Jerry Glover before whale exhibition

▲ Me and Bird watching whales, San Ignacio Lagoon

▲ Bird Baker

▲ Touching my first friendly gray whale, Mexico - 1983

▲ Eye to eye with a humpback whale

▲ Now he turns the air on!

▲ Good friends Mark and Debbie Ferrari - Whale Researchers

▲ Me diving with green sea turtles off Maui

▲ Painting with dolphin Kibby, Florida - Dolphin Research Center

Painting lifesize breaching Humpback Whale, Honolulu, Hawaii - 1985

SKY CLIMBER   R D WERNER

▲ Seeing Honolulu Wall in 1980 for the first time
▲ With Ilikai Marina building manager Marge McDowell
▲ Finished Whaling Wall 6, Honolulu, HI - 300 feet long x 20 stories high - April 22, 1985 - Ea

▲ Waikiki Beach - 1980

▲ With my attorney after judge saves Honolulu Whaling Wall

Extinction of Whaling Wall - Honolulu

With Tom Selleck

▲ Celebrating completion of Whaling Wall 6

▲ First Whaling Wall in Funabashi Japan, Tokyo Bay

▲ Painting first ceiling wall in
Yamagata, Japan

With good friend Tamaki ▶

Completion of "Orca Heaven," Yamagata, Japan - first ceiling mural

Mr. Kawada at special dedication ceremony, Yamagata, Japan - 1990

Brother Bill at work

▲ Brother "Bobber" Bill diving
Great Barrier Reef, Australia

▲ With friend Mike Peak, Australia

▲ Down under in Sydney, Australia - 1990

▲ Blank Lahaina Wall

▲ Proposed Lahaina Mural rendering 1983

▲ Historic Lahaina Whaling Wall - 1990

▲ Whaling Wall 33, "Planet Ocean" by Wyland - Guinness Book of World Records - May 4, 1

116,000 square feet, 1,280 feet round x 110 feet high - 7,000 gallons of paint

▲ Whaling Wall 50 - Atlanta, Georgia - 1993 - East Coast Tour

▲ Team Wyland Crew - East Coast Tour 1993 - 17 Murals, 17 Cities, 17 Weeks

(from left to right) Top row - Daemon Clark, Erik Hansen, Carlton Clark, Roy Chavez, Tom Wyland, Mike Murray, Fred Mongeon, Greg Scha
Bottom row - Trish Clark, Valerie Wyland, me, Angela Eaton, Sondra Augenstein, Jim Augenstein, (not pictured, Randy Hunter)

▲ With friend Jimmy Buffet

▲ Mayor Roy Chavez

▲ With Ted Danson - American Oceans Campaign

▲ With wildlife artist Robert Bateman at dedication of Whaling Wall 13, Victoria B.C., Canada

▲ Finishing lifesize Right Whale, Atlanta, Georgia - 1993

7
Michelangelo Painted On His Back

...If you don't make any mistakes it doesn't take long...

WYLAND

Three years after I had painted my first Whaling Wall in Japan, I was asked to return and paint a private mural in Yamagata. This wall was actually to be a ceiling that overlooked a giant swimming pool in an exclusive resort. I was intrigued by the idea of doing a ceiling, and I was intrigued by the fact that this was to be a private mural for which I was going to be paid very well.

I had been introduced to a big developer named Mr. Kawada, or, Mr. Kawada-san, as he was called in Japan. His daughter and her husband had made the introduction in Hawaii, and Mr. Kawada flew us to Japan, first-class. I was traveling with my younger brother, Bill, president of Wyland Galleries in Hawaii. It was his first trip to Japan, after which he and I were to fly directly to Australia to paint

129

two more Whaling Walls and dive The Great Barrier Reef.

After arriving in Tokyo, we took a bullet train to Yamagata. The entire trip was high-profile and "first cabin." When we got to the resort, I asked immediately to see the ceiling. What I saw was amazing — an awesome display of workers were finishing a maze of scaffolding that literally covered the entire floor of this cavernous indoor pool. The scaffolds went right up to the ceiling, where I would be able to reach up and paint it. I was very impressed with the overall size and shape of the ceiling and the fact that the sides had no corners — it just kind of rounded out. I immediately had a vision of the swimmers in the pool looking up into this ceiling as it would be from a diver's perspective, about 60 feet deep, with this refracting light coming through the surface and several orca whales swimming overhead.

This was the first time I had tried to paint the underside of whales. I had painted numerous murals by that time, but I had never done a ceiling before. I kept thinking about Michelangelo as I wondered about how I was going to do this. I had no problems painting on any scale and was absolutely confident I could do it. But I didn't know how long it would take or exactly what it would involve.

Michelangelo Painted On His Back

I started the next morning painting in giant masses of ocean and blue color, using hundreds of gallons of blue paint. Although we had masks, it was very intoxicating to be right under the spray gun, and I had to continuously climb down and run outside for some fresh air. It was like a big blue fog in there. Many of the dozens of workers assigned to help me ran out and didn't come back, so Bill and I were like the last two survivors. We just stayed in there and kept spraying and spraying. The cloud of paint was so thick I could hardly see. So I had to just keep envisioning the entire painting in my mind's eye.

Aside from having to weather this great blue storm, this part of the painting was no problem at all — I was moving along swimmingly. After I painted the ocean water, I assumed I would paint the lifesize orcas the same way I had painted whales in my other murals. I started to ghost them in. But what was happening was I couldn't really see them because I was too close to the ceiling. When I got down on the floor and looked up, it was a terrible mess. They were all out of proportion — upside down, sideways and backwards. My whole perspective was off. I then began to appreciate Michelangelo even more. It was looking to be an impossible painting. I have to admit, looking back, that I was really nervous. Here I was getting paid a lot of money to do this mural, and I was having a horrible start. It was alright until I started sketching in the whales. Then it became like a nightmare.

I went up again and tried to paint after seeing it from the floor, but it was the same problem. Perplexed beyond belief, I was standing there thinking about what to do next when Bill walked up holding two yardsticks taped together with a brush on the end. "Why don't you try this?" he said. "Lay on your back like that Italian guy. You know, what's his name — the one who painted on his back."

"You mean Michelangelo?" I asked.

"Yeah, lay on your back and sketch it in."

Now, my brother ain't no art scholar or museum curator, but he was aware of the "Agony and the Ecstasy" and, as it turned out, had looked up at the ceiling long enough to develop an appreciation of his own as to what Michelangelo had to contend with. I thought it was ridiculous, but I had run out of ideas of my own so I tried it. I laid on my back and, lo and behold, found that the distance between me and the ceiling allowed me to see the whale I needed to sketch a lot easier. Not only had I never painted a ceiling before, I certainly had never laid on my back to sketch or paint. I had always done everything freehand; to me, this was cheating. But Bill was exactly right. I decided quickly that this was okay because I had no other way of doing it, and because he and I would be the only ones who would ever know.

I sketched out the first whale and, from then on, it was just a matter of painting in the lines, like a coloring book or painting by the numbers. I painted the first orca very quickly and then sketched the second whale. By the time I got to the third whale, I didn't need to sketch it. I could stand up and go back to doing it freehand.

But the credit goes to Bill. I couldn't have done it without him. Of course, I didn't tell him that. I didn't tell him he had saved the Japanese ceiling. The flow of advice I would have to live with if I did tell him would have spewed out of my brother faster than the paint he had helped me spray on the ceiling. I told him to go out and play golf.

By the second day, I was getting close to finishing the mural. I was happy things progressed so quickly, and the mural was beautiful. I felt pretty sure Mr. Kawada was going to like it. But it was going *too* fast. To stretch it out a little longer so Mr. Kawada would feel like he got his money's worth, Bill and I would sneak out and play golf in between the painting. They had this incredible golf course, one of the nicest in the world, and we had free rein because the resort wasn't completely open at the time. We would play 18 holes each, sometimes 36, and still had time to finish the mural in three days.

On the sixth day, Mr. Kawada, the owner, flew in for a special dedication. We had to kill two days before he arrived. The first thing he said when he walked up was, "I understand that his mural only took three days." He looked more concerned than amazed. "Why did it take only three days?"

I looked him straight in the eye and, through my interpreter, said, "Well, if I make mistakes, it takes six days." I was holding up three fingers to illustrate. I guess it didn't occur to me that this man had not become a multi-millionaire businessman by not knowing how to count to six. "But," I continued, "if I don't make any mistakes at all, it only takes three days."

When the translator said this to him, Mr. Kawada got a big smile on his face and laughed out loud. "Great!" he said, suddenly looking up at the mural. He said he loved it and asked if I would return to Japan to do more for him. I told him I would, but that he had gotten off cheap this time. I said the next time it would really cost him. Of course, I was feeling my oats a bit. This was the most I had ever been paid for a mural, by far. The bottom line was that Mr. Kawada was very happy, and so was I. For a little while, I had lived what Michelangelo had lived. It felt great!

In fact, the press had started calling me a "Maritime Michelangelo" right after the dedication ceremony. It was flattering, but the only thing I could think of was all the difficulties the great master must have had. I had just learned that it was one of the hardest things to do — painting a ceiling. When you're that close and painting something large, your entire perspective changes. Even on my back, it was not the same as just standing back from a vertical surface.

Mr. Kawada felt so good about the mural that he invited us to fly back to Tokyo with him in his private helicopter, a high-tech aircraft that was out of this world. He flew us back and paid us, paid all of our expenses, everything. He was just incredible. For a brief moment, I guess we gained a little against America's trade deficit with Japan.

8
Down Under with Brother Bill

...If you happen to see a whale, it is only because they want you to...

WYLAND

7 hope you as a reader will indulge me for a few pages while I quickly recount an experience I had with my brother, Bill, while we were in Australia. Some of you may find it humorous. Others may not. But I think you'll all agree it borders on the ridiculous.

First of all, Bill and I had not been roommates since elementary school, and even then it wasn't good. I grew up with three brothers — I was the second oldest behind my older brother, Steve; Bill was two years behind me; and then there was Tom, our youngest brother. Bill and I are probably the most alike, outgoing and sort of hyper if you know what I mean. But, we found out we had dramatically different lifestyles during a trip "down under" as we were once again thrust together as roommates.

Whale Tales

After painting the ceiling mural in Yamagata, Japan, Bill and I boarded a plane from Tokyo to fly directly to Sydney, Australia. We were then to fly to Bundaberg, a city known for its great rum and as the beginning of the Great Barrier Reef. Some of the city's officials there had seen my work in Hawaii and in other places and decided that I should come to Bundaberg and do a Whaling Wall. At the same time, the Sydney Aquarium had asked me to do a mural for them. This was an opportunity to paint my first two Whaling Walls in the Southern Hemisphere.

So Bill and I took this long flight. I forget how long, but it was long, including a few stopovers like Hong Kong and some others. In most cases, when I do a free mural, the city or sponsor donates the food, the accommodations, transportation, the whole nine yards. Bundaberg did not exactly have a big budget, but I felt it was important to do some murals in other countries, and I was interested in Australia and the opportunity to experience the Great Barrier Reef. Bill had recently become certified in scuba diving, and we were going to try to do some diving between painting.

A good friend of mine, Michael Peak, a cameraman for NBC in San Diego, had some vacation time and was going to meet us in Australia to document the painting of the mural. Only he arrived a day early and, to my surprise, had already settled into one of the rooms we had reserved. Somehow in the confusion, the room I was supposed to have by myself now became the scene of a roommate reunion with my brother. It was a reincarnation of our boyhood bedroom and, as I would find out, a reincarnation of Bill's boyhood. It was a small room, with only one bedroom, and one of us to sleep in the living room. We're talking very tight quarters here. Anyway, there was a lot of pressure on me because I had to paint a very large mural. And ol' Bill, well, he was on vacation. Of course, he was looking around for business opportunities as well, but primarily he was there to enjoy himself. For me, I had to paint two walls in Australia. So right off the bat, there were two different agendas going.

With neither one of us thinking, we just threw our bags in the room, and Bill claimed the back bedroom while I ended up in the living room. That first night should have sounded an alarm for me to re-pack my bags and go out and camp on the beach. Number one, I like total peace and quiet when I sleep. The only thing I want to hear is the ocean. Bill, on the other hand, has to have the TV blaring really loud. In fact, if Bill is sleeping, no matter what time of night it is, and the TV gets turned off, he'll wake up immediately and say, "Hey, turn the TV back on." So the first night was quite an experience, and we went back and forth about having the TV on or off and arguing about who was going to do what. Eventually, I won the battle that night, and we turned the TV off. I can't say for sure, but I don't think Bill had a very good night's sleep that first night. It was to be my last victory.

Then came the real awakening — morning! I like to sleep in to 8:00 or 9:00, but Bill is up at the crack of dawn. He was up at 6:00 and, of course, on goes the TV. I was still pretty groggy from the last mural in Japan, but he's up and at 'em and already on the phone, making his calls. I suppose all of that moving around and jabbering on the phone urged him into the bathroom, and I swear I didn't see him for well over an hour. I'm not sure what all went on in there, but he took a *National Enquirer* in with him and just did not come out. By 8:30, I was up and supposed to be at the wall at 9:00 for a press conference. I knew I was in trouble when I saw water seeping out from under the bathroom door and into the hotel room carpet. I had no idea what was going on. As far as I knew, there was only a shower in there.

"Hey, get out of there! I've gotta be at the wall at 9:00!" I yelled at him, banging on the door. Finally, the door swung open, and there he was in all his glory. If he had let his breath out, the towel that barely reached around his rotund belly would have sailed across the room like a kite. Now it was my turn to go in and use the bathroom. I walked in and was shocked to find water lapping at my ankles. There was a lake on the floor. Every towel had been used. The entire roll of toilet paper was wet. And the mirrors — shaving cream all over, hair everywhere, toothpaste squirted all over the water fixtures on the sink. I'm telling you, the John Candy and Steve Martin scene in *Planes, Trains & Automobiles* was mild compared to this. The *National Enquirer* was glued to the floor. It was just unbelievable.

"What the hell?!" I yelled out. There wasn't even a towel or washcloth. So I composed myself and asked him if he wouldn't mind, please, going to get me a towel.

"Sure, just a minute," he said, as if nothing at all was unusual about laying waste to a bathroom right before someone else entered. I came out of the shower soaking wet and there he was, with the determined towel still stretched across his torso, watching TV.

"Hey, get your fat ass off the bed and go get me a towel!" I yelled. Running out of time, I couldn't wait for him to roll off the bed and get dressed to go out and find me one. So I scrounged one of my T-shirts out of the suitcase, wiped myself down and hustled off to the wall.

This went on for a week—seven days and seven nights. The bathroom, the TV and, I forgot to mention, his snoring. The roof was absolutely caving in. I don't snore. I sometimes talk in my sleep and that may have driven him nuts, but this guy was snoring and everything else—all kinds of body noises coming from him. I was throwing stuff at him—pillows, whatever I could find nearby in the dark. The only thing I could do was try to go to sleep first.

One night, a girlfriend I knew from Australia wanted to come over and spend some quality time. I had pre-warned Bill. Of course, he was propped up in his regular position with a beer. I said, "Bill. . . I kinda got some company coming over tonight, this gal I know, a diver. We'll probably get together, so would you mind going down to the pub and getting LOST for awhile?"

"Oh yeah, yeah, no problem," he says, agreeing to leave the moment she got there. Well, Lisa, a divemaster from nearby Lady Elliot Island, showed up with some anticipation of having some private time with me. She walked in and sat on the bed next to me and 'ol Bill, who was still propped up there watching TV. I gave Bill the nod at that point and turned my attention to Lisa. I don't know if he was in some kind of trance or something, but he didn't quite get my meaning and just sat there on the bed like a toad on a wedding cake. This went on for about half an hour! When you've got a beautiful woman sitting next to you, half an hour feels more like three days. I don't know what program he was watching, but he had this stupid look on his face like, "Huh? What are you talking about?"

Finally, I just said, "Get the hell out of here! Get lost! We want to be alone!"

"Oh, okay, why didn't you just say so," he said, rolling off the bed and eventually making his way out the door. At last, I thought, as Lisa and I sat there talking. Fifteen minutes later, BOOM, BOOM, BOOM on the door —he's back. I don't know about Bill, but it takes me a little longer than 15 minutes. I mean I didn't even have my shoes off and there's my brother, banging on the door. I opened the door a little, with the chain still on. "What?!" I whispered through the crack.

"You finished? I'm kind of tired," he said.

"You've only been gone 15 minutes!" I whispered again, a little louder this time.

"Well, it was kind of a rough bar."

"I don't care if it's a jail," I said. "I don't care if it's San Quentin. Get your butt out of here! Go get lost for awhile!"

"Okay," he said with a sad little voice as he walked away. Half an hour later we hear BOOM, BOOM, BOOM on the door again—he's baaaack. This went on like all night. It was unbelievable. I had to get rid of him three, four times. It wasn't very romantic.

"Didn't I tell you to get lost?

"Well, I've been gone an hour."

"No, it's only been half an hour. Look at your watch. Don't come back until 11:00. You got your watch on?"

At 10:30, it was BOOM, BOOM, BOOM again. He had a key, of course, but I had the chain up. I finally let him in, and he went into the back bedroom. I don't know, but it was very uncomfortable having your brother back there, and the bathroom was in the main part of the room. So, really, nothing was accomplished. My brother was basically ruining my lovelife. I'm sure it wasn't good for him either, not too exciting. I was pretty boring. I like to go to bed early. I usually try to sleep a good nine hours, and he only sleeps a few hours a night. It was pretty hilarious.

Now, don't get me wrong. Bill's my brother, and I love him. He's a very jolly fellow. But I swore that week I'd never, ever, room with him again. Diving with him was no treat, either. We eventually had a chance to go out and dive the Great Barrier Reef, about a two-hour boat ride from Bundaberg. It's one of the greatest dives in the world, just fabulous. I wanted to spend a lot of time underwater in Australia so I could reflect the reef's marine life in my murals and later in my paintings.

Our dive group consisted of Lisa, Mike Peak, myself and "Bobber Bill." We called him that because he just could not get underwater. Mike still tells stories about that dive trip. Lisa and I were buddied up, and poor Mike had the pleasure of diving with Bill. Of course, Bill always blamed his superhuman buoyancy on the equipment — it was never his fault. I probably should have warned Mike that Bill was a new diver. But so was Mike for that matter. Only, unlike Bill, he didn't fall asleep in class.

Lisa and I headed for the bottom, and Bill kicked like hell to join us. But he was kicking with a full BC and wasn't going anywhere. About 30 minutes later, they continued to stay on the surface, Mike hanging with him as his "buddy." Bill didn't know how to deflate his BC, which is kind of a vest that keeps you floating when you're diving. So he blamed everything on the BC. Mike finally went over and helped him. Then Bill's mask was foggy. He was having problems with his mask. At that point, I hadn't seen them down there so I came up and traded masks with him. Bill finally got under a bit, but then shot right back up to the surface, due of course to his equipment. Actually, he had pushed the "INFLATE" button on his BC again. He rose to the surface so fast he breached. I had seen whales breaching for many years, but this was the first time I'd ever seen a human clear the surface. I couldn't be sure, but I think I heard someone yell, "Thar she blows!"

It was a nightmare dive for Mike because he had to stay with him. Lisa and I had a great dive. Mike's last statement to me was: "I will never, ever, dive with Bobber Bill again."

Meanwhile, back in Bundaberg, the Whaling Wall was coming along nicely. I remember thinking that if I could get my brother out of the bathroom in the morning, I could probably finish this thing on time. I depicted The Great Barrier Reef in the mural, along with humpback whales swimming in their breeding ground there, a loggerhead turtle and a lot of other fish.

The mural was 85 feet long and 95 feet high, and probably the best part of the trip was when I finished it about 5 p.m. The city wanted to have a special lighting ceremony, so I had to race back to the hotel, get ready and try to get back to the wall by 7 p.m. When I left the mural, all was well. It was a normal day in Bundaberg. When I went back, there was a major traffic jam. I mean there were 5,000 people there. The police had blocked off the roads, and there was a giant throng of people in the streets beneath the wall on the main street. People were partying and very festive. Later, I found out they were there for the wall, to pay homage to and celebrate their new landmark.

The city had announced they were going to light the wall that evening for the citizens. So they had set up a flatbed truck for me to stand on and make a speech when the mayor presented me with the key to the city. It was quite a ceremony. When I got out of the cab, the police recognized me and escorted me to the flatbed truck because there were so many people. As we began to move through the crowd, there were some cheerleaders shooting off poppers. They shot one at me, and it went over my head and hit Mike right in the eye. I remember he fell to the ground, holding his eye and yelling, "You got the wrong guy — I'm not the artist!"

I turned around and looked at him and said, "What happened?" He just kept saying, "They got the wrong guy." He was sort of half-heartedly laughing, but he said it really hurt. We made it up to the stage — brother Bill, myself and Mike — and joined some really good speakers who talked about how nice it was for an American to come down under and paint this mural. I was showered with gifts. It was really an emotional night. This wasn't even the dedication, this was just the lighting of the wall. I thought, "My God, what's gonna happen at the official dedication?"

The entire City turned out to celebrate the lighting of the wall. To this day, it is the most memorable reception I've ever received. The following day, we dedicated it at a very large ceremony again. That night, our last night in

Bundaberg, I managed to get some rest. We were to fly the next day to Sydney to start another mural, and I started talking to Mike and Bill about how I needed rest that night. This naturally led to a discussion about how my brother and I had such a hard time as roommates, and Mike just shrugged his shoulders and suggested that we get another room.

"They're only $12.00," he said, not quite understanding the stunned looks on our faces. Bill and I looked at each other and in unison said, "SHIT!" It never occurred to us during our week of playing the odd couple to simply go down to the office 30 feet away and ask for another room. We both tried to run to the door at the same time to get to the office first. We pounded on the counter, saying, "WE NEED ANOTHER ROOM! NOW!"

"No problem, mate," the concierge said.

The people of Bundaberg gave us a very nice send-off the next day. It was an hour or two by air from Bundaberg to Sydney. Bill and I had decided at that point that we had already done our duty — our roommate duty — and that no matter what the cost, $10,000 a night or whatever, we would have our own rooms in Sydney. We laughed about it later. But, at the time, we were ready to go nose to nose.

Whale Tales

I went on to paint the wall at the aquarium at Sydney's Darling Harbor, and Bill flew directly over to New Zealand by himself — a little holiday; he had been working so hard. The Sydney mural was on the inside front entrance of the aquarium. When you first walk in you are confronted by two lifesize humpback whales. The whole time I worked on it, I was saying that the best wall would have actually been the roof. I had painted a ceiling, and now I was looking at the entire roof, which was over 450 feet long and 150 feet wide. It was highly visible because there was a bridge that went over Darling Harbor, and everyone who visited there, millions, would look right down on the roof of the aquarium.

I proposed the idea to John Burgess, the director of the aquarium, and he was very excited. He, in turn, proposed it to the City Council, which seemed to respond quite well. But, all of a sudden, the architect got involved and was opposed to it and it became a major controversy. In fact, *Good Morning Australia*, a program just like *Good Morning America*, had come out to do a story on me, and I had them on the roof. I envisioned an entire pod of blue whales and was telling them how beautiful this roof would be as a rolling ocean.

This vision was a little too much for the architect, though. He wouldn't even contemplate painting over his roof. To me, it was another opportunity to enlighten the people and show them the whales.

I told them I could paint both murals while I was there, but they couldn't get the approvals fast enough. The architect had a lot of clout. I hope one day to go back to Darling Harbor and do that roof. As one of the most visible walls in Australia, it's still pending and do-able, and I still want to do it. Bill and I met up after I finished the wall in Sydney, and we flew back to Hawaii together, laughing all the way about our roommate escapade. All in all it was an incredible trip, and we painted two beautiful murals.

9
Painting Murals in the Dark

...Everyone always asks how long it takes to complete a painting...
I say, this year it took 37 years...Next year 38...

WYLAND

*L*ahaina is a city rich in whaling history and, in recent years, whale research. For me, it was a calling I had decided to experience as fully as I could by moving there and setting up camp. My reading and everything I'd heard about it had drawn me to this small island town in the middle of the Pacific. I had arrived in an historic whaling village that had become one of, if not the, most renowned whale watching ports in the world.

I was there to study the great humpback whale and paint. My plan was to find a nice little studio within a few weeks, a studio that, considering my limited resources, would definitely have to double as my home.

A lady friend of mine had picked me up from the tiny airport in Kaanapali and, after a short drive, we pulled onto

Front Street, the main thoroughfare in Lahaina Town. The buildings lining both sides of the street were rustic, but freshly painted and bustling with the energy of the tourist trade. Every other storefront, it seemed, bore a shingle identifying it as an art gallery or a shop selling everything from scrimshaw and jewelry to T-shirts and shave ice. Of course, there were a variety of restaurants to choose from as well.

As we drove down Front Street, I saw an open seawalk that looked over Lahaina Harbor and the ocean. At the end of the walk, straight ahead of me, there was this wall literally rising out of the water. It wasn't particularly large, but because of the seawalk, it was visible from almost every vantage point along the busiest portion of Front Street. By that time, 1980, I had traveled through a lot of cities and looked at hundreds of blank walls for potential canvasses. This wall impressed me because of its visibility and unique position right on the water, but I wasn't planning at that moment to ever paint it. I was just looking.

We stopped at the Pioneer Inn, a old hotel dating back to Lahaina's whaling days. I wanted to stay there because the old whalers had stayed there. I wanted to absorb all the history I could. Also, it was the cheapest place in town at $20 a night. I had put together enough money for a week or two worth of nights. I enjoyed the inn immensely. It was right on the water, with a restaurant and a great rowdy whaler's bar downstairs. Lahaina and Maui were absolutely infectious — very warm and alluring, the perfect artist's paradise. Each day I found myself walking along Lahaina Harbor and looking out at the water trying to imagine what it must have been like in the early days. It was a dream come true to actually be there and experience this village first-hand. I hoped the feeling of the place would later be reflected in my work.

Initially, I spent a lot of time just sketching and drawing, and hadn't set up to paint yet. I met some people from a dive shop who took me diving off Lanai, an outer Hawaiian Island that faces Lahaina Town. The divemaster took me on an "intro" dive to a reef called Cathedrals. We encountered an number of green sea turtles and other marine life, but what stuck in my consciousness was the light from the surface. There were these lava tubes, and the light would pyramid through these tubes forming an effect that looked like stained glass. It was very spiritual, thus, the name Cathedrals. I was hooked. I couldn't afford to get certified until a few years later, but I dived all the time anyway. A group of friends I met later invited me to go out with them whenever they had an extra seat. Molokini Crater was one of my favorites, and Molokai. I began to look at the undersea in a completely different way, and this would later be seen in my work. My paintings would become more realistic and start to capture the real spirit of the ocean and what's beneath it.

It was November when I stayed at the Pioneer Inn, and all of Lahaina was excited because the following month the first humpback whales would be finding their way to Maui to mate and calve. I figured I was in the right place at the right time. I was breathing in everything I could from this island called Maui. Islanders call it "Maui. . . No Ka Oi," which means "Maui. . . the best." And it was. The sunsets were awesome. I couldn't think of a better place to be on earth. I had found my new home.

The time had come to find a more permanent place to live, so I inquired about some studio space above a dive shop. It was a tiny room, renting for $150 a month. But it was the only thing available, right next door to Greenpeace, directly across from the Pioneer Inn and the Banyon Tree. It had no bathroom or shower. There was a bathroom down the hall, but I had to share that with both the dive shop and Greenpeace. And I had to go outside and bathe with cold water from a garden hose. I would hose myself off every morning when the sun was up to keep me warm. I'm talking some humble beginnings here. I lived like this for a couple of years. Fortunately, Maui is warm most of the time.

So I had my studio. It was small but cozy and had a great view of Lahaina Harbor. A friend of mine, an artist named Andrea Smith, who had gone to the same art school I went to back in Detroit in the '70s, gave me a little futon to sleep on. We had the same painting instructor, Russell Keeter, and it was good to have someone from Detroit I could bond with. Andrea, whose art was starting to sell on Maui, also loaned me an easel and gave me the lowdown on the local art scene. Her husband, Gary, and their family were very supportive, and I'll always be grateful they were there in the beginning to help me.

From the window in my studio, I could see the Pacific Ocean in the front, and a portion of the West Maui Mountains from the side windows. It was a million-dollar view from a $10 room. The next step was to start painting and earn a living. I had already discovered that Hawaii was a much more expensive place to live than on the Mainland, and I had begun to live on Snickers candy bars. I managed to barter a painting for some initial art supplies and a few canvasses from a local guy named Ted, who owned a small art supply store in Lahaina, and started to paint. I've always been fairly prolific as a painter, I guess, and I quickly covered a good number of canvasses. Now I had to sell them.

I didn't really have to bathe myself for two years with a water hose. I found a creative way to get all of the paint off me at the end of each day. There was an old hotel down the street called the Lahaina Shores that had a swimming pool and a jacuzzi. It became my ritual each evening to stop painting around 6:00, put on my sneakers and jog down to the Lahaina Shores to watch the sunset. But the sunset was only part of it. I was one of those painters who got more paint on himself than on the canvas, and some of those oils didn't come off easy. By the time I hit the hotel property, I would be pulling the sneakers and my socks off and, without breaking stride, jump right in the middle of a jacuzzi full of people. My blue fingernails — hell, blue paint was all over me — never failed to generate conversations about whales and my work as an artist. Most of these people were tourists and wanted something special to take home from Maui. I would invite them to come over to my studio the next day, and many of them took me up on it. I sold more paintings out of that jacuzzi than I ever did out of a gallery in those days. I saved all my money and reinvested it in more art supplies. Eventually, the studio was so full of paintings that I was forced to go out and find a gallery to represent my work.

This was a special time for me. The art movement in Lahaina was starting to take off, and Maui would soon become one of the major art markets in the world. My paintings were very inexpensive then. You could get a large oil for around $150. The same painting today would cost around $20,000. Like Lahaina, I felt I was ready to take off. I found a gallery on Front Street called the Dolphin Gallery. The owner, Steve, was very pleasant, and the gallery had a lot of wall space because it mostly carried jewelry and sculpture, which worked out well for both of us. I used to paint at the Sawdust Festival in Laguna Beach, where I would put my easel in front of my booth and let the public watch me. I always felt good about meeting people and talking about my art. Most artists prefer to paint by themselves but, since it didn't bother me, I learned that painting in public was a very successful way to market your work. I enjoyed being accessible; it was fun. I would set my easel up right on Front Street in front of the gallery, and it was a big hit. We began to sell quite a bit of art, with the gallery, of course, getting most of the money. I was starting to be well received and was making a name for myself. I painted in the studio during the day and, in the evening, in front of the gallery. I was talking to people constantly and still doing my sunset jacuzzis. At 23, I was an energetic young artist making a modest living in exactly the place I wanted to be.

I should probably mention that there was another guy in Lahaina painting whales at the time. His name was Robert Nelson, a young painter who had Lahaina Gallery, the largest gallery on Maui, sewn up with his work. With the gallery's help, Nelson had created a hot marketing scheme claiming he was the founder of the "above and below" scene, that is, painting a marine scape from both above and below the ocean. He was saying he painted the first one in 1979.

First of all, this whole notion that he was the first to do an "above and below" painting was ridiculous. In fact, it was embarrassing. Many artists had done "above and be-low" for years. I had first seen the technique in the early '70s in *National Geographic*. The only difference was that there were numbers next to the fish in the magazine. I, myself, had done "above and below" since 1971, but was never pretentious enough to claim I started it. I was aware of many artists who had painted the "two world" scenes, some dating back to the 14th century.

Anyway, I was just starting out and had a lot of ideas about what I wanted to do. For one thing, I already felt successful because I was living my dream of being a working artist. If I made a lot of money, great; if not, that was okay, too. A few years later, I decided to leave the Dolphin Gallery and, with my brother, Bill, open my own gallery and market my own work. I wanted to represent myself and control my own destiny, control how my work was merchandised and sold. I wanted a more family-style gallery.

I was lucky to have the support of some other artists in Lahaina, particularly Andrea Smith, Andrew Annenberg and many others. I was, at the time, still working to get approval for my first Whaling Wall in Laguna Beach. But the wall at the end of the seawalk on Front Street kept haunting me. It was just large enough to portray a lifesize humpback breaching out of the water, a scene I had seen many times off the shores of Maui. I simply made up my mind that this was the perfect canvas, and the perfect place, for a Whaling Wall. I had discovered through my Laguna experience that the media could be an invaluable ally in garnering support for a public mural. After talking to Phoebe Gedge, the owner of the building, and receiving her approval, I announced to the media that I was going to paint this wall. *The Maui News* sent Lynn Horner, one of their writers, out to interview me. She wrote a large feature that carried a full-page spread of photos of me barefoot in my Front Street studio, plus a rendering of the wall with the complete mural. It was an inspired article, entitled "In Search of the Perfect Wall," published on May 13, 1983. Friday the 13th — good thing I'm not superstitious. At that point in time, this would have been my third Whaling Wall, having completed the first one in 1981 in Laguna Beach, and another at the Orange County Marine Institute in Dana Point, California. The story generated a great deal of support among everyone I talked to. The dye was cast.

A couple of days later, however, my phone rang, and I

heard the voice of a man named Jim Lucky. I had heard this name a few times before. He was the head of the Lahaina Restoration Society and was heavily involved with the Lahaina Historical Society. He was, you could say, a Lahaina heavyweight — the guy who, I was told, ran Front Street. He asked me if I would drop by his office to talk to him about the wall. I told him, sure, but I was nervous. What kind of person runs a whole street? The whole thing seemed kind of eerie. I had visions of Lee J. Cobb in the movie, *On the Waterfront*. Was he going to have my legs broken if I refused to do what he wanted?

Well, he wasn't a gangster, but he thought he had that kind of intimidation going for him. He was a big, heavy haole guy with a loud aloha shirt and a large kukui nut lei around his thick neck. I had seen him on TV promoting the Cartheginian and other things — truly a legend in his own mind. I sat down in front of his huge desk and opened my portfolio for him. I was sharing with him what I wanted to do when he abruptly interrupted me and blurted out, "Look, I run Front Street," in case I hadn't heard of him. "Nothing gets done in this town without my permission, and this Whaling Wall will never happen. I don't care if the entire state says you can do that wall, I'll take you to court personally and stop you."

I didn't want to go to court for a mural, but I was relieved that it sounded like I wasn't going to have to wear casts on my legs. "I understand your perspective," I told him diplomatically. "But I've already painted it."

"What do you mean?" he spurted. "What are you talking about?"

I had already had enough of this jerk who considered himself some kind of kingpin just because he had lived there longer and was a high-ranking member of a couple of local society groups. "I've already done it in my mind's eye, and there's nothing you can do about it," I said rather defiantly. "I think it's important for Lahaina. It's going to make a major impact on the people who visit here, and it'll represent the challenge we have of protecting the whales."

Mr. Lucky stood up, and we were nose to nose. After a moment, he relaxed a bit and declared, "You're serious, aren't you?"

"Yes," I said through gritted teeth. "It's worth whatever it takes to do it. I've already been through the politics of doing one wall in Laguna, and I'm definitely not afraid of you."

"You know, Wyland, don't take this personally," he said, softening. "I really appreciate your work, but not on Front Street."

I left his office feeling pretty lousy. I went to talk to the City, but Lucky had already talked to them and infected them with his viewpoint. He said the mural would upset the historical character of Lahaina Town. I guess no one ever enlightened him that history is a record of, among other things, how a town like Lahaina developed its character, and of how that development would never have occurred without change. You can't just stop history in its tracks. It's ongoing. It's being written at any given moment, and will continue to be written in the future. This mural, I felt, would depict not only Lahaina's whaling history, but its current history of whale protection. Whale watching had replaced whaling, and people would now be able to see a lifesize humpback breaching off Lahaina 365 days a year, a natural, I thought.

It was going to be the same thing I had encountered in Laguna Beach — entrenched residents who didn't want their city to change anymore. I had a lot going at that point and decided it was best to just back off awhile and let it rest. I let it rest for several years, in fact. One night, I was sitting around with some other artists — Andrea Smith, Andrew Annenberg, Piero and several others — and said, "What do you all think about us going over there one night and just painting that wall?" They all laughed at me, but I was dead serious. "Look, there are four or five of us here. I'll go up and sketch it in and number all the sections. Each of us can take a part and paint it."

Again, they laughed it off as too many beers for Wyland. But I never forgot the idea. Then, in 1987, I sent a complete package to Mayor Hannibal Tavares of the County of Maui. He called himself "Hannibal the Cannibal," a nickname I presume he hadn't earned through experience, but one can never be sure. I went to his office, and he told me if I wasn't nice he'd eat me! I figured Lucky had talked to him about our little face-off a few years before. An experienced politician, the Cannibal told me he appreciated my art and what it was doing for the whales, and he thought I definitely should do a wall in Maui. But his idea of public art and mine were two different things. He asked me to paint the mural on the third floor inside a building behind a secretary's desk in

Painting Murals in the Dark

Kahalui.

The County's planning director, Chris Hart, had a better understanding of what public art was and told me they wanted me to paint a wall, anywhere except Lahaina. Sounded to me like he'd been talking to Lucky. Again, I was stonewalled.

Nine years after I had first tried to get permission for the Lahaina wall, I was starting to gain a pretty good following. I had completed the wall in Waikiki, which became one of Hawaii's favorite landmarks. I had moved to the North Shore of Oahu. And I had completed 29 Whaling Walls throughout the United States, Canada, Japan, Australia and Europe. I was painting the first of two walls in Kapaa, Kauai, when I started thinking about Lahaina again. I had actually never stopped thinking about it. The Kapaa mural was on a clock tower and, as I painted a humpback breaching across the Na Pali Coast, I kept looking at the clock and thinking, "It's time for conservation. To hell with politics!"

I came down off the tower and told my volunteers to get the leftover paint to Maui immediately. Without any fanfare, I flew over and quietly checked into a small hotel. After nine years, I had made up my mind that the only way I was going to get to paint this wall was to paint it in the middle of the night. I had with me Mike O'Brien, a professional painter from Kauai who had volunteered on my last wall. And, at the last minute, I told a few others to join us at the Lahaina seawall at 3 a.m. The Lahaina bars would be closed and the traffic minimal. Mike had the scaffolding ready for me and was priming the wall when I arrived about 2:45. I wondered how I was going to do this in the dark. If I had planned better, I would have waited for a full moon. It was pitch-black out there, and I could barely see the wall. But I had painted this mural in my mind's eye so many times I could have painted it blindfolded.

There was nothing historical about this wall. It was nine years old and made of T-1-11 wood siding, the same as my new garage. Plus, it had been painted sort of a turd-brown color. My crew was getting noisier as we got busy, and I was nervous about the police showing up and charging us with painting graffiti on the wall. I have to admit, I was stimulated by the fact we were challenging the system. I always figured that if the system didn't get challenged, it would eventually become corrupt. Jim Lucky was living proof of that. I said to myself, "If artists aren't going to challenge the powers that be, who will?" I had a shit-eatin' grin on my face the whole night. I knew I would be subjected to substantial opposition from the Lahaina "Hysterical" Society, but I felt in my heart that the vast majority of people supported our efforts to paint the first Whaling Wall in Lahaina.

Again, the problem was no light. Actually, there was a tiny sliver of a moon and one little streetlight helping us out. I told my crew to quiet down and stop being so rowdy; they had brought beer with them to bolster their courage, I guess. There was definitely some electricity in the air. I remember thinking that this must have been how the old whalers felt when they came into town in the middle of the night and were ready to howl. Well, we were definitely ready to whale!

I grabbed my spray gun and loaded up the first colors and started ghosting in the West Maui Mountains, blocking in some of the ocean and eventually ghosting in the whales. The painting materialized very rapidly, faster than any mural I'd ever done. I was working on pure adrenaline. The sun would be up soon, and I had a decision to make: either I was going to finish the wall and get the hell out of there and let them try to figure out who did it, or just paint into the day and dodge the bullets.

As the sun began to rise, I couldn't believe my eyes. The mural was right on the money. It was perfect. Perfect proportions, perfect colors. It was a Godsend. The lighter it got, the more beautiful it looked. I decided, what the hell, and stayed around to paint in more detail. A huge crowd started to gather and seemed to love it. I was expecting the shit to hit the fan any minute, but it didn't. Everyone watching looked to be as inspired as I was by the great humpback breaching out of Lahaina Harbor, with the old Pioneer Inn and the West Maui Mountains in the background. Suddenly, a beautiful rainbow appeared across the mountains to my left, and I quickly added it to the mural. Then, something happened that sounds so fantastic that many people I tell this story to have a hard time swallowing it. But it's true, and the hundreds of people lined up on the seawalk saw it just as clearly as I did. A *real* humpback, honest to God, suddenly breached out of the water in almost the exact position as the whale I had painted on the wall. It was absolutely breathtaking! The throng of people watching me paint actually broke into a cheer at this miraculous sight. It was, in the truest sense I can imagine, a vision of life imitating art. Later that afternoon, a lady who'd been rolling her baby in a stroller on the seawalk came up to me with her eyes wide with amazement. "My baby has never said a single word — not mama, not daddy, nothing," she said. "But he just looked up at your wall and pointed his finger and said "WHALE! I can't believe it! I just can't believe it!"

Neither could I. But, why not? The entire morning was shaping up to be a miracle. I had just painted a large mural in almost complete darkness, almost like it had painted itself. Then a whale breached out of the water right in front of the wall as if it wanted to celebrate this tribute from mankind. Why shouldn't a one-year-old baby boy find himself as awestruck as the rest of us and decide that very second he could talk? I was so pumped up I was ready to believe anything could happen. I no longer worried that Lucky and his boys, or the bureaucrats from the County, would try to stop me from finishing. They wouldn't dare try to contaminate this moment. There were just too many people present who were, as I was, completely caught up in the celebration of this inspired painting. I was so bathed in euphoria that I painted all day and into the next day until I finished it late

Sunday afternoon.

The mural was an extension of the marine history of Lahaina and all of the color that went with it. What had been a dull brown wall had been transformed into a vibrant painting that captured the spirit of the place, eliciting support from all who viewed it. It wasn't until Sunday afternoon that I heard anything even remotely resembling a negative comment. I was finishing the detail on some of the whale's barnacles when a long Cadillac pulled up with its tires almost on the sidewalk. I could hear an older lady screaming something at me through the large car's half-open window, but I couldn't make out what she was saying.

"Excuse me?" I said, trying to be polite. I always try to talk to anyone who comes to watch me or visit me when I'm working on a project, and I usually can talk to them from the scaffolding. Then the lady rolled her window down all the way so I could hear her better.

"Do you have permission to paint this wall? she screeched again. "Who gave you permission?" When she saw that I wasn't even going to respond to her belligerence, she peeled away from the curb, glaring up at me until she had to turn her eyes back to the road to keep from hitting the parked cars along Front Street. Of the hundreds of people who watched the mural being painted that morning — tourists, locals, young and old — she was the only negative person we encountered.

The sun was setting off Lanai when I put the final barnacles on the humpback. I was out there meeting people and talking to them about the mural when I heard things like: "This is great! What an improvement;" "This is the best thing that ever happened to Lahaina;" and "This is the only thing FREE in Lahaina." I had finished Whaling Wall 30, and the following day, Monday, January 21, 1991, we held a special dedication ceremony. Two well known Hawaii residents, John Pitre, the surrealist artist, and Jerry Lopez, the legendary surfer, officially dedicated the mural. A Hawaiian priest said a beautiful prayer and blessed the mural and the whales, taking a ti leaf and scattering sacred water on the wall. The water was carefully contained in a wooden bowl, from which the priest slowly dipped it out. He finally decided to throw the entire koa wood bowl of water onto the wall at once, spraying everyone with holiness thanks to the strong wind blowing in from the harbor. We all felt the special spirit the mural possessed and its important message.

173

Whale Tales

As I was talking with some reporters afterward, I was rudely interrupted by a man named David Assaire, a member of the Lahaina Town Action Committee. With a very loud voice for the benefit of the press, he started asking me if I had permission to paint the wall, and who I thought I was to come paint a wall in Lahaina without asking anybody. Now that I think about it, that must have been his mother in the caddie the day before. This jerk was attacking me openly with over 200 of my supporters all around him. Evidently, he wanted his name in the paper really bad. And he got what he wanted. The reporters went ahead and flocked to him, listening intently while he told them I had painted the mural without a permit and that I'd intentionally done it over Martin Luther King weekend. What that had to do with it I don't know, but I've always admired Martin Luther King and was honored that I had created an important piece of art during a holiday held in his name.

I knew who was behind this. Mr. Lucky had sent his lackey to disrupt the ceremony and tell the press the mural was illegal. Lucky, himself, didn't have the balls to come down and face me himself. When the reporters turned to me and asked for a response, I told them: "I have permission."

"From who?" the lackey boomed.

"From God," I answered. "He's the only one I need permission from."

I guess Maui's two local newspapers didn't buy the permit from God thing. They were owned by the same people and did a 180-degree turn. The glowing positive articles turned overnight into sensationalized exposes that accused me of everything from painting a billboard, a ridiculous charge I had already defeated in court in Honolulu, to not being from Maui. My attorneys had looked at the County's laws and ordinances and found nothing that said there was a law against public murals. They found ordinances against billboards and signs, but nothing against murals. I had permission from the owners and lessee of the building, and I had waited nine years for permission from the County, which I didn't see was anywhere near being forthcoming. This was the only way I was going to get the wall done, and the vast majority of Maui's residents were behind it. In fact, we circulated a petition and gathered thousands of signatures from Maui residents in favor of the mural, with only a handful against it.

I spent the next year defending the Lahaina Whaling

Wall. Eventually, the Maui County Council held a public hearing. It was supposed to be a fair hearing, but *The Maui News* did a story featuring the views of each of the Council's nine members, five of which said they were going to vote against the mural no matter what. They clearly had no intention of listening to a thing I had to say. They attacked me unmercifully, with the help of some other artists in Lahaina, who accused me of painting the mural just to promote myself and my galleries. It was all utter nonsense, but the Council voted unanimously to have the mural removed and started fining me $100 a day until I did it. They thought I was just going to paint over the wall but, to me, the word "remove" meant something entirely different. I had a friend of mine, a building contractor named Richard Oliphant, actually remove the wall, panel by panel, and replace them with new wooden panels and paint it the same turd brown it had been before.

I still have the wall in storage and ready to be re-erected as soon as Lucky and these politicians are swept out and replaced with people who have a little more vision and appreciation for what this mural can mean to Lahaina. We'll even have a re-dedication ceremony. This wall was a gift to the people of Lahaina, but a few decided to reject it and give it back. This was not the Hawaiian way. It was not the human way. It was just special interest politics rearing its ugly head again. They had to win at any cost. The local media had hit an all-time low, again. The way I look at it, they may have won the battle, but not the war. I'm still young and will continue to paint Whaling Walls throughout the world, where they are received with only the highest of accolades. Lahaina is the one town that has shunned one of my walls, but only temporarily — I never give up. I was asked how long it took to paint this mural, and I can honestly say it took nine years and three days. It'll be back up where it belongs one day, and that day won't come soon enough for me!

10
Painting the Largest Mural in the World

...The larger picture is not only can we save the whale,
but can we save our oceans, our planet, us...

WYLAND

I was painting in my Hawaii studio one morning in 1991 when the City of Long Beach, California, contacted me about the possibility of doing a Whaling Wall in their fair city. The mayor, city planner, and other members of the community had invited me to have lunch with them as soon as I returned to the Mainland, on the *Queen Mary*, the famous cruise vessel that had adopted Long Beach as its home port. I was to meet all of the city's VIPs in the ship's main dining room, where they wanted to discuss their proposal with me. Flattered and curious about the offer, I accepted and ate a wonderful lunch at a very nice table with about 40 Long Beach city officials, all attired in their best business suits and looking optimistic about the possibility of having me paint a wall for them. After we ate, they took me topside to look at the City of Long Beach from one of the higher decks of the *Queen Mary*. The vantage point had been carefully selected so that we were looking over what I would later find out was the Long Beach Sports Arena and Convention Center.

As I looked out the window, I saw this giant, round cylinder that appeared to be more than 10 stories high. It was huge, the largest wall I'd ever seen. I immediately commented, "There's a perfect wall right there."

"You got it!" they said in unison. This was the wall they wanted me to paint; it was already planned. They had seen the wall I had completed earlier in the year on the Edison Building in Redondo Beach, which was quite large, and at the time, the largest mural I'd ever painted — over 600 feet long and 10 stories high. They'd selected a structure almost three times the size of that wall so they could one-up their neighbors in Redondo Beach.

I suddenly started to share their excitement and asked them where we were on approval to paint the center. They confidently told me I had just had lunch with everyone who was needed to grant permission. All I had to do was say "yes," and tell them what I needed. I couldn't believe it. I had been through so much red tape with my walls in the past, and here was the entire City, their decision-makers at least, telling me all I had to do was give them the word. There was no way I was going to pass on doing a Whaling Wall this big, especially if the permission process was already taken care of. I told them I'd donate my time, but that I'd need the paint, the scaffolding and a number of other things and that I'd get back to them. I did, however, ask if I could have a tour of the wall. We loaded into some cars, drove over and got out for a long stroll around the massive 360-degree convention center. The outside was 110 feet high and 1,225 feet in circumference. It was tiring just to walk around it. The building had been there for 30 years, and no other artist had ever conceived of such a mural. In fact, people were already talking about it being the largest mural in the world. Indeed, we found out later it exceeded the Guinness Book of World Records' largest mural ever by over 24,000 square feet.

I was pretty confident I could paint it, but I would need a tremendous amount of support from the City and enough time, materials and volunteers. As I looked at the wall, I began to envision a theme of Southern California marine life, depicting the many whales, dolphins and other indigenous sea life. The idea that the convention center sat right on the water and, in fact, very near the *Queen Mary* and the Spruce Goose made it that much more attractive as a site. It meant that a great number of people would be exposed to the wall, which, to me, was a very exciting possibility.

I decided I would do it, and we scheduled to paint the wall in the spring, after I returned from spending the winter at my home in Hawaii. Not long after I returned to Oahu, however, the whole thing erupted into a major controversy. I had felt from the beginning something was wrong; it all sounded too good to be true. It seems the City kind of back-doored the project and didn't involve all segments of the Long Beach community. The Art Association of Long Beach was extremely irate that they'd been passed over without being consulted. So I was getting slammed from this organization, which had incited the media to join them in calling foul. Like a wildfire fanned by the hot Santa Ana winds, a circus of propaganda and misinformation swept through Long Beach. Having been told that day on the *Queen Mary* that the City had done its job and cleared the way so I could come in and paint, I had already scheduled the two months I thought it would take to complete the mural. I was locked in, and now they were caving in big-time. I found out later that was the way the City did business in Long Beach, and what had looked to be unnecessary resistance from a local art association might actually have been the City's fault in the first place. Regardless of origin, I was once again being used as a scapegoat, a community group's vehicle to grind an ax and attack its city administration.

Over my fax machine, I began to receive articles and political cartoons that had appeared in the Long Beach print media. I had seen some politics and red tape before, but nothing on this level. It was ugly, ugly, ugly. Nonetheless, I was still gung-ho about doing the mural when the architect came out of the woodwork and declared that the convention center was minimalist architecture, and that my mural would ruin it. I immediately thought, "minimalist architecture? This thing is an eyesore. It looks like a giant oil drum sitting next to the harbor." When I stated this to the City, they laughed and said they felt exactly the way I did.

I had been through these politics before and had developed fairly thick skin. But to be honest, things were getting very shaky, and the City was ready to throw in the towel.

The Art Association's main argument, which included new twists from week to week, was that they felt any Long Beach art student could do the mural. They pointed out repeatedly that I wasn't from Long Beach and who was I to paint the largest mural in the world. Their beef wasn't about the project itself, per say. It was about who should paint it. They suggested there be an art contest among art students since anyone could paint whales on a wall. It astounded me how little a group of people calling themselves an "Art Association" knew about public murals.

"Well, anyone can sing a Dan Fogelberg song, but Dan Fogelberg wrote the song," I said at the time, adding that this mural was "my song" and that I was determined to do it. "This wall has been here for 30 years — if anyone could paint it , then why haven't they?" I asked. While they were scratching their heads for an answer, I told them the reason they hadn't painted it was because it was next to impossible. No mural had ever been painted on this scale, and even I was having a few second thoughts about being able to accomplish something this large. But I was up to the challenge and committed to finding a way.

The City finally informed me that they couldn't get any

funding because the City Council had said earlier that the mural wasn't going to cost the City anything. It was the opposite of what I had been told. Like Redondo Beach, they would finance the project, donate the paint and scaffolding and get as many volunteers as I needed. Now they were saying they weren't even going to be able to donate one dollar. The entire financial burden was unexpectedly hoisted onto my shoulders. Not only would I have to paint the largest mural in the world, I would have to supply the paint, the scaffolding, all supplies, everything.

As terrible as this was, I decided the wall was still worth doing. Sinclair Paint sold me the paint for cost, which ended up costing over $50,000 out of pocket — my pocket. The wall first had to be washed and prepared; that cost another $30,000. And the other costs, the tools and scaffolding, was another $50,000. By the time all was said and done, it cost me nearly $200,000 of my own money to do this mural. Plus, I had blocked out eight weeks for the project, which kept me from painting in the studio and cost me even more. Had it not been for the success I was enjoying as a fine artist, there was no way I would have been able to do this mural.

By then, the City had all but given up when my brother,

Bill, and my mom received a call saying that one final meeting would be held on the mural. Bill stood up at the meeting and said he would write a check for $10,000, and my Mom said she would match it. This was very generous of them, by the way, since I was unable to attend and both checks, I would find out later, were to come out of my account. They were both too embarrassed to tell me about it. I got a call from the City that afternoon, saying the wall was on and that they'd raised $20,000. I didn't find out until later that my own family had put up the money, my money, so the City could say they were donating the paint and supplies.

The wall was a go, again. I thought, you know, $20,000—that's a good start; that's respectable. Anyway, the time came to fly over to Long Beach and get started. I wasn't scheduled to start painting until the following day, but I decided I would drive by the project. When I got to the wall site, I found total chaos, total mayhem. People were choking each other on the ground and swearing at each other, throwing things; it was raining; paint was dripping; it was complete craziness. There were probably 20-30 volunteers without a clue as to what was going on, and no one to supervise them. It was outrageously out of control.

Painting the Largest Mural in the World

The moment I got there, the scaffolding guy, announced he was quitting. "I'm done. I've had it. I'm through," he said. The City was supposed to have additional volunteers there to help prime and paint the wall, but no one showed up. The only guy who remained faithful was my old friend, Roy Chavez, who had helped me on the Redondo Beach project. He was the chief painter for Southern California Edison and a die-hard Wyland fan. He was a professional, but he was starting to panic because it was such an immense job and he wasn't getting any support. Roy had already re-cruited his wife, Nancy, to help because they couldn't get an-other painter. I assured him I was there to run things now and that I'd make sure this project would be done at any cost. So he calmed down — I mean, he looked like he was going to have a heart attack.

I pulled Roy and Nancy off the wall and gathered the volunteers we had left for one of my Vince Lombardi pep talks. Somehow, the fact that I had finally arrived started to make everyone feel better; they were saying things like "We can do it, we can do it." But it wasn't quite that simple. We had to re-group and really sit down to figure out strategi-cally how to do this huge project. I gave up all ideas of checking in at my home in Laguna before returning the next day to start the mural. I just dropped my luggage and got up onto the scaffolding with Roy and started painting. From that point on, we worked six weeks straight without taking even one day off.

The first thing my team had to do to prepare the wall was to pressure-wash it with high-powered water. That was quite a job because they had to go up on the scaffolding and blow off some of the old paint. Then they had to tape up all the windows, which took close to a month. I knew going in it was going to be quite an effort, and I was more than right. Fortunately, our labor pool would grow to 200 volunteers, from the vice-mayor to street people to everyone in between. My policy was, and has always been, to never turn anyone away. If they wanted to be involved, I found a way. I figured if they were involved and volunteering like I was, then they'd be committed to it. But we had so many volunteers, I couldn't get anything done. Eventually, we managed to get organized with a paint crew, an office crew, an office mom, a scaffolding crew and an equipment crew. The scope of this project was unequaled by any I'd known, except perhaps Cristo's running fence.

Painting the Largest Mural in the World

By the time we were really ready to roll, the media started coming out in droves and everything broke loose. Somebody decided a smear campaign might be in order and sent out brown envelopes to the media with photos of me painting nude portraits of women. The photos had been cut out of a men's magazine, which, in 1976, had published a photo spread of some nudes I'd painted. The accusation accompanying the torn out photos was that I was going to paint nudes, not whales, and that I was painting the wall while I had my shirt off. This whole sordid attempt at sabotaging the mural was quickly sensationalized by the media. And when *The Los Angeles Times* came down to talk to me about it, I yelled at them from the scaffolding: "Before I talk to you, are you from *The Los Angeles Times* or the *National Enquirer*?"

I could not believe it at first. Was I the only artist in the world who had ever painted pictures of nudes? What about Michelangelo? What about all of the masters? Like many artists, I had painted nudes all the way through college. It was critical to my training that I paint the human form. To attack me for it was absurd! But the press had something that added more color to the story, a more sensational angle.

Even the mayor was quoted as saying the photos were pornographic. I finally had to just laugh it off, and the whole stupid uproar quickly faded into yesterday's news.

I initially managed the start-up of the project myself, but finally had to bring in my entire staff to assist in the effort. One of the challenges we didn't expect was sorting out who among the volunteers was qualified. And, believe me, we went through some major knuckleheads. When you have an open door policy like that, anyone can come in and, boy, they did. Then, just as we got started, the head of the Arts Commission paid us a visit. At first, I was confrontational and repeated what I had said earlier: "Hey, if any art student can do this, why didn't they? You had 30 years to do it. You have no idea what the hell you're talking about, so get lost!"

When they turned around and walked away, however, I thought better of it and called them back over. "Listen, I don't know what your politics are with the City," I said, "but you don't even know me and I'm trying to do something nice for Long Beach." I think he had recognized what we were really up against. It was not an art school project for a student. We basically shook hands and moved on. There was no time for nonsense. We had a job to do and a world record to achieve! And it took every single person we had to do it.

The paint was brought in by the semi-truckloads — 7,000 gallons, more paint than I've ever seen, enough to fill several storage rooms. I was wondering how I'd get most of it up on that wall. It was really intimidating, and the more I looked at the wall, the more I questioned whether I could actually achieve this. Roy, though, was constantly at my side, teaming up with other professional painters to prepare the wall with a good coat of epoxy primer. When this was done, and the primer dried, Roy and I began painting massive bands of background color on the wall. There were probably 12 different bands of color that had to be applied around the entire circumference — all 1,225 feet. It took a lot planning and organizing. But most of all, it was just plain old-fashioned hard work. By the second day I couldn't even lift my arm up I had sprayed so many gallons of paint. I'm sure one of these days I'll develop Carpal Tunnel Syndrome. It was unbelievably physical. Most of the time, it was very, very hot outside, but it did rain. We just painted in between rain clouds, just kept pumping hundreds and hundreds of gallons of paint across the wall.

Whale Tales

It was about this time I found out that the $20,000 the City claimed it had raised was actually my money. I was absolutely livid. I had hired a new secretary, Sylvia, who, on her first day at work, accompanied Bill and me to meet with the city manager. The Vice Mayor, Jeff Kellogg, who eventually worked as a volunteer on the wall, was there as well, as were several other city officials. So I was in a meeting room at City Hall with these suits, and the city manager told me I was on my own as far a funding is concerned. Here I was spending 13-14 hours a day, seven days a week, creating a gift to their city, and they had not raised a dime. In fact, they wanted to throw the entire bill at me and, on top of that, had the gall to tell me they wanted me to donate some of the proceeds from the sale of my artwork to a few of their city projects.

I went off the Richter scale. I literally got right in the city manager's face and told him he was a liar and that if he thought I was going to give the City one more penny, he could shove it up where the moon don't shine. I was fed up with their bullshit and I just lost it. "I'VE DONE EVERYTHING FOR LONG BEACH, AND THEY'VE DONE NOTHING BUT HARASS ME!" I yelled at him, pounding on their big table and throwing one whale of an artist's temper tantrum. Sylvia, the shy young lady that she was, simply stared at me with her mouth open. Her first day on the job, and her boss goes berserk. Bill, who had seen me like this before, tried to slip out the back door, but I screamed at him: "GET BACK IN HERE!"

When I feel like I'm getting screwed, I don't pull any punches. I was ready to kick the shit out of this city manager for lying to my face. Luckily, Jeff Kellogg stepped in and reminded them that I was doing the wall for free and was paying for everything, and that I'd already donated $70,000 worth of my artwork to various charities in Long Beach. "As far as I'm concerned, he doesn't owe the city anything," Kellogg said. Everyone in the room looked sheepish, except for the city manager. He and I seemed destined to have bad blood between us, I guess. He had tried to blackmail me into giving more money, and I had given all I was going to and was calling him on it. Now I understood why the Art Commission was fed up with the City.

Above all of this rage, however, was my vision of seeing the wall completed. I try to do what I say I'm going to do, and I wasn't going to let this two-faced bureaucrat throw me off. It was time to get back to work. Eventually we had painted enough sections that I could start painting the marine life. When I got that first whale on the wall, it seemed like the spirit of the entire city changed overnight. Even the media, those self-appointed analysts and chroniclers of society's highs and lows, began writing positive stories. Reporters and cameramen started coming down to the site and seeing for themselves what a tremendous effort it really was, not only by me, but by the volunteers. They also saw that the only reason I was working without a shirt was because it was so bloody hot.

About one week into the mural, I had painted several whales, and we were getting a lot of attention. The following weekend the Grand Prix was scheduled to begin, and the race route would go all the way around the mural site. Over 200,000 people were expected to attend the event, which meant that 200,000 people would be able to see this Whaling Wall being painted. The crew from ABC's *Wide World of Sports* came up and asked me if they could do a segment on my work. "Absolutely," I told them, and right in the middle of the Grand Prix they split off to do a feature on my work, with highlights of me painting the mural. They also aired footage of Al Unser coming up on the scaffolding and painting a small blue whale with me. I ended up naming that whale "Little Al."

The race promoters had asked me not to paint during the Grand Prix, but I insisted that I had to complete the mural in a certain amount of time, and they backed off and let me paint. I had the best seat in the house for the race, too. Roy and I sat up there and watched the race and took breaks to paint. It was the closest thing we would have to a rest until after the mural was finished. They had also asked me if I wanted to be a celebrity driver in the Grand Prix. I told them I wanted to, but that I had to finish the mural first. No one knew who would finish the mural if I crashed, so we agreed I could do it the following year instead. During the race, the Whaling Wall received national and international coverage. When Danny Sullivan, who edged out Al Unser to win the race, was at the press conference, I presented him with one of my bronzes. "That was a whale of a race," I told him. To me, this was an unlikely but effective vehicle to promote whale conservation. There were a lot of people sitting there watching the Grand Prix who were going to be sensitized to the plight of the whales. I was intrigued by this chance to inspire them, even if they happened to be sitting in their living rooms with a six-pack watching the Grand Prix on TV. For the most part, these folks probably had never been exposed to whales in their environment. I felt like I was giving them that opportunity.

I had completed a California gray whale section — an entire lifesize pod migrating. And during the Grand Prix, I finished a family of blue whales — a mother, her calf and their escort. I also painted myself in the mural, which was the first time I'd done that. The idea wasn't just to paint myself, but to show a diver so people could see how large these creatures are. When people watch me paint a lifesize whale, they can see how we compare in size. But I wanted this to be a lasting reminder, so I painted a self portrait of me diving right next to a blue whale. I painted myself in full dive gear with all the detail, right down to the tattoo I have on my left arm that says, "Wyland." We then went on to paint a pod of orca whales. All these whales are indigenous to waters off Southern California. About midway through the mural, we started calling it Planet Ocean, which seemed to be the perfect title because it signified how important the ocean is to the Earth.

Painting the Largest Mural in the World

At some point, I had hoped to give everyone a day off. But I knew that to finish we would have to stay pumped up and paint continuously. We would start painting at 7:00 or 8:00 in the morning and continue until 6:00 or 7:00 at night, seven days a week. As I painted all the way around the arena, I kept looking around the curve in the wall for the place I had started. Six weeks later I found the other end. The curvature of the wall was interesting in that it presented a unique challenge. If I was painting a blue whale, I would be painting the body and not be able to see the head or tail. I had to envision the entire whale in my mind's eye. It was like an out-of-body experience — while my body was up on the scaffolding, my mind's eye was on the ground looking at the entire wall. I liked the way everything turned out, though. The roundness gave the mural more of a three-dimensional quality, a never-ending painting.

It was not all smooth sailing as we neared completion, however. In the fifth week, news of the Rodney King verdict suddenly invaded every television screen in America. As soon as the verdict came down, the riots started and immediately a guy on a motorcycle was murdered very near the wall. As I painted on toward the end of that day, there were many fires and gunshots near the Convention Center. We could see the fires clearly from the scaffolding, and there were bullets literally flying over our heads. To say it was unnerving would be an understatement. It was downright scary. It seemed like the whole city was ablaze.

Throughout the project, I had a major art exhibit by the street, in front of the mural site. During the riots, there was a lot of looting going on, and the police pulled up and told us the rioters were heading our way. They told us to do something about the art and run for cover. I didn't hesitate in coming down off the scaffolding, and my crew and I started grabbing sculpture and paintings. Just two blocks away, the looters were breaking windows and stealing property. Someone was yelling, "Save the whale art!" I could see my entire life's work being taken. Fortunately, the Convention Center was opened up for us, and we were able to put my art under lock and key.

The sun was just starting to set as the crew and I sat around and drank a few beers to settle our nerves and wait out the quiet before the storm. Surprisingly, the area around the Whaling Wall turned out to be one of the quietest and safest places in either Long Beach or Los Angeles. There were a good number of us, maybe 100, reflecting on the mural and its message of peace. The whole world had its eye on the cities of Los Angeles and Long Beach that night and, as we waited, it occurred to us that if people could somehow learn from the whales and dolphins how to co-exist in peace and harmony, we wouldn't have these problems.

On this night, though, we were scared for our own safety. The police were dispatched to protect us and escorted us to our hotels. Mine was right across the street at the Sheraton. In the evening, we didn't leave our rooms for fear of dying. There were ambulances, police cars, sirens. You could see buildings burning from my hotel room. How strange it was to be involved in such a peaceful environmental mural when the environment around me was so violent and hostile.

We locked ourselves in our rooms every night for three nights, but the storm never really came. During the day, I had to get out there and paint. On one hand I felt safe, but on the other, I felt like a pretty good target. Here was this little white dude up there painting a mural — a juicy target for anyone with a scope on their gun. I didn't think anyone was going to shoot me, though, and I kept on painting.

Whale Tales

Someone gave me a hat that read: "Kill an artist, Go to jail."

I finished the wall the night the riots ended. We had a special dedication ceremony and my friend, Chris Robinson, the actor, dedicated the wall, along with Vice Mayor Jeff Kellogg, who had supported me and worked so hard on it. The mural was, for me, my greatest challenge. It was not only the largest, but it required the most perseverance and stamina. It took everything I had to complete this wall, but it was definitely worth it. On the day of the dedication, the head of the Guinness Book of World Records presented me with a certificate, certifying that this was indeed the largest mural ever painted. For several days, I couldn't wipe the smile off my face, and everyone who had worked so hard to complete this wall had the same problem. We were a family of dedicated volunteers who shared a commitment to raise awareness through public art and education.

Looking back on it, I would do it again, and I probably wouldn't do it any differently. Sometimes you have to go through these things to really appreciate them. I still enjoy going down to Long Beach and to the *Queen Mary* and seeing this mural. I'm hoping that when they finish the new additions to the Convention Center, they'll add some plaques along a walkway or something that'll describe the marine life painted on the wall, and provide some scientific information. This mural has been filmed, photographed and seen throughout the world, and it continues to be one of the most visible landmarks in the world.

I remember looking at it from my hotel room when it was finished. I could see the giant white circular roof of the sports arena. Ever since, I've had thoughts of going back and breaking my own world's record and adding to that mural. With seven-eighths of the earth covered by water, the earth is, by any definition, a water planet. I'd like to illustrate this by painting the top of *Planet Ocean* with a view of earth from space, tying it into the sides, making it an even larger mural. Wouldn't that be great?

It's no big thing.

—————————— **U . S . A .** ——————————
EAST COAST TOUR • SUMMER 1993

Portland, ME
June 1 - June 7

Portsmouth,
June 8 - June

Boston, M
June 15 - June

Providence, R
June 22 - June 28

New York, N
June 29 - July 5

New London,
July 6 - July 12

Philadelphia, PA
July 13 - July 19

Wildwood, NJ
July 20 - July 26

Wilmington, DE
July 27 - August 2

Washington, D.C.
August 3 - August 9

Baltimore, MD
August 10 - August 16

Norfolk, VA
August 17 - August 23

Wilmington, NC
August 24 - August 30

Myrtle Beach, SC
August 31 - September 6

Atlanta, GA
September 7 - September 13

Sarasota, FL
September 14 - September 20

Key West, FL
September 21 - September 27

11

17 Murals, 17 Cities, 17 Weeks

...If one kid grows up to be another Cousteau,
all my efforts will have been worthwhile...

Wyland

I had put off painting murals on the East Coast for five years, since 1988, in fact, when a friend of mine named Steven Katona and I first talked about doing a series of Whaling Walls along the Atlantic Seaboard. At that time, I was actually in Deer Isle, Maine, to visit another friend of mine, singer/songwriter Dan Fogelberg. I had heard about a whale researcher at the College of the Pacific and went to visit him — it was Steven.

We hit if off immediately, even though he was a scientist, and I was an artist. We talked a lot about that, how science and art have always been at opposite ends of the spectrum. And we decided that my murals, which depict lifesize whales and marine life that are anatomically correct, represented an opportunity for science and art to work together to accomplish something bigger. As I was leaving, Steven autographed his book on whales and dolphins, planting the seed: "Looking forward to your East Coast tour. . . Steven Katona — 1988."

It made a lot of sense. The Atlantic Ocean is very important, and I've always wanted to paint its vast array of marine life. Besides, I was starting to receive a lot of invitations from some of my collectors who live along the Atlantic to paint Whaling Walls in their cities. Finally, one evening, I was sitting in my living room with my assistant, Angela Eaton, and Sondra Augenstein, my special events coordinator, and her husband, Jim. "Why don't we just do it?" I said to them. "We can make one trip and do them all — just get it over with."

So we started looking for a map of the United States, and the only one we could find was a tiny map Sondra tore out of her day-timer. The map had all the states, but it only showed a few cities in each one. Now, maybe this wasn't the most scientific way to go about it, but the cities we selected for the tour were those lucky enough to have had their names listed in this little day-timer. We later added Washington D.C., Philadelphia and Sarasota, but this, believe it or not, was how we chose the other 14 cities. Sometimes, that's how it works in the art world.

I must have been out of my mind to think we could attempt this project — paint 17 murals, in 17 cities, in 17 weeks. But when we were looking at that little map, it looked pretty achievable. We all looked at each other and just said, "Let's do it!" Personally, the whole thing offered me an exciting challenge. It gave me an opportunity to top the largest mural in the world, which I'd painted the year before.

First, we needed money. And we needed donors for our paint and other materials. This was such a formidable task that I didn't know if we could get it all together before the tour was scheduled to start. In fact, I was beginning to think we should wait until the next year. Fortunately, we got such an overwhelming response from all the cities we contacted that we were encouraged, and somewhat committed.

It was a good thing we had Sondra to set this tour up and remove all the roadblocks and obstacles we encountered. She did more than remove obstacles — she bulldozed them and took no prisoners. Normally, it would take over a year or more to gain approval to paint a mural in some of these cities, but Sondra blasted through the red tape and politics in a matter of months. Without her, we wouldn't have even gotten off the ground. We also contacted every single person we knew and sent a newsletter to all my collectors, asking them to assist with the project. And they responded beyond our expectations.

As a precursor to this marathon, we embarked on a whirlwind press tour that was pretty phenomenal in itself. We visited all 17 cities, from Portland, Maine, to Key West, Florida, in only 14 days. It was like a rock tour. In most of the cities I'd only have a few hours to spend and, in some of them, they hadn't even found a wall yet. I remember when we hit Rhode Island, the city officials hadn't found a site, so I loaded them up in our van, took them out on the freeway and found a wall for them.

"Hey, there's a wall right there," I said. "Pull off the freeway; let's get off at this exit."

"Well, we haven't talked to that person yet," the city official pointed out.

"Don't worry about it; we'll go talk to him now," I said.

"Well, what if the owner's not there?"

I mean, it was like "what if, what if." But I felt something about this wall was special as we pulled up to the building, which housed some kind of machinery shop. I noticed right off there was a Cadillac, a brand new Cadillac, blocking the loading zone. "The owner's there," I said to myself. "Only the owner would park there." We piled out of the van with these guys looking at me curiously, and I marched the eight of us into this poor guy's office. We were greeted by the receptionist, the owner's daughter, and I introduced myself. The city official gave her his card, too. I guess he thought we needed a little extra credibility. The daughter-receptionist called into her dad's office and, after a short conversation, informed us that her father was into whales and had some in his office, and he wanted to know if we wanted to come in and see them.

This, to me, was a miracle. In fact, the East Coast Tour became known as the "miracle" tour afterward because a number of things like this happened later. We went in and met Joe and Doris Cassiere, who owned the business and the building. We had talked to Joe less than 15 minutes when he told us he liked the whole idea and that it was fine with him. The city officials could not believe this was happening. They'd never seen anything like it. To me, it was just another day at the office.

Just before we were to start the tour, I did a huge art show in San Diego, and thousands of people showed up to send us off. That same afternoon, I painted a mural depicting humpback whales on the side of a brand-new tractor trailer that had been donated by National Van Lines. They also provided me with drivers, Carlton Clark and his wife, Trish, who owned the truck and drove it all the way to the East Coast and throughout the tour. I loved the idea of this mural traveling all over the country. The idea was to expose as many people as I could to the beauty of these whales, and what better way than to take them on the road, literally. I mean, how many people are going to be thinking about whales as they travel down the highway? I think this mural changed Carlton and Trish's lives; the attention they've since received as traveling Wyland ambassadors has been tremendous.

We arrived in Portland near the end of May, ready to whale. The media came out in droves. Mike Venema and Kathleen Rogers, my publicists, did a fantastic job. The press coverage — local, national and international — was phenomenal during the entire tour. But we had a little delay in

Portland, as we stood around under our press tents watching a cold, hard rainstorm pelt the city all morning and into the afternoon. I finally got sick of waiting and ran out onto the pier and did a dance — a non-raindance. People thought I was crazy, but — and I know this is going to sound like I made it up — after 15 minutes, the rain stopped. I know what many of you are thinking: "Jeez, this guy thinks he's some kind of wizard or medicine man." Well, I don't know anything about that kind of stuff. All I know is that we had scheduled six days or less to complete each of these 17 murals, and we were desperate to get this one started. Call it luck, divine intervention or just a simple break in the weather, it stopped raining. We wasted no time thinking about it. Our volunteers immediately climbed up and wiped down the wall, and we started spraying paint.

Before we even flew out from California, I had contacted Steven Katona and asked him to be my consultant on the types of whales, dolphins, seals and other marine life that inhabit the Gulf of Maine and the coastline of the northeast. I wanted to paint the marine life that was found near each of the cities we would be visiting. On the Portland wall, which was 1,000 feet long, I painted a humpback whale and her calf, finback whales, minke whales, white-sided dolphins, Atlantic bottlenose dolphins, some sea lions and a logger-head turtle.

When the mural was half-way done, the crowds were getting larger and the city felt it was important we get some security — if only to keep the people away from me so I could work. We had created quite a frenzy. It was all very friendly, but it was becoming increasingly hard to paint because the crowd wanted autographs and to talk. I've always enjoyed that part of it, but the reality was that we had a huge wall to complete. They hired a personal security guard for me to kind of keep the crowds back. His name was Roger — a very nice guy. At the same time, my brother Tom, a professional bus driver in Portland, and his wife, Valerie, were on the tour with us. Tom was driving the cherrypicker scaffolding and doing a lot of my personal driving. As a professional, he took a lot of pride in his driving ability.

Roger was trying to make sure the crowds were staying back for a lot of reasons, some of them being safety. Traffic still needed to drive past the wall. He was leaning down to talk to some of the people in a passing car when my brother,

Tom, who was driving the very heavy cherrypicker lift, which had a large arm and bucket, accidentally backed the entire rig over the back of Roger's ankle. Roger, of course, started screaming at the top of his lungs, which got our attention. I yelled, "Stop! You're on his ankle!" Tom stopped the rig immediately, but it was too late. He'd already snapped the back of my security guard's ankle and leg in about seven places. The heavy rig was still balancing on the back of his leg. My brother, for some odd reason, always went right when I said left. And when I said right, he would go left.

Finally, I yelled, "Get off his leg, go left." For the first time, Tom turned the correct way and backed off his leg. If he had gone the other way, I don't think Roger would have a leg today. This poor guy then had the composure to take his radio out of his pocket and call himself an ambulance. He wasn't mad; he was just embarrassed by the whole thing — but not as embarrassed as my brother. As Tom and I knelt down to console him, he said he was glad because now instead of watching the crowd, he could watch the mural being painted. In fact, Roger followed the tour for many more cities. He had some vacation time due to the cast on his leg.

Whale Tales

We teased Tom about Roger for the entire tour, he being a professional driver and all. The fact was that we had a cast of the most unusual bunch of characters that ever ventured into the unknown. I likened it to this: When I selected these people to go on tour, it was very similar to a whaling captain in the old days when he used to try and entice men to join his crew. He would say, "Come and visit exotic ports, three square meals, women, wine". . . It was recruiting, heavy recruiting. I fancied myself as much more than an Army, Navy or Marine recruiter. I was of the days of the whaling captain, enticing my crew to travel along on this voyage of exotic adventure and pleasure and big bucks. Of course, none of it was true. The reality was 14-hour days, seven days a week. I always say there's no rest when you are on planetary duty. And that, simply, was what it was — hard work and no rest. It made me think I might have been an old whaling captain reincarnated. Maybe I had once been a whaling captain and this was my payback — to have to do something for the whales in my new life. I don't know — there were a lot of similarities.

Regardless of whether or not I had been a whaler in a previous life, my first mate on this voyage was Roy Chavez.

We call him the "Mayor" because he runs the painting activity around each of the walls we paint. Roy has been painting with me since I painted the Redondo Beach wall in 1991. Ever since we painted that wall for Southern California Edison, where Roy works, he's been hooked. He has declared that he will continue to paint with me wherever and whenever I ask him. Without Roy assisting me in painting the background, and preparing the walls and running my paint kitchen, it would be impossible to do anything on this scale.

There was one night, though, I could have done without him. The Mayor was teamed up with Greg, a real odd couple relationship. These guys were both married, and both had mustaches. They were roommates, buddies, the Roy and Greg show. These two characters were sleeping one night, and Roy had to take a leak. So he reached up in the dark for the light switch and inadvertently pulled the fire alarm switch instead. The entire hotel went crazy as all of those fire trucks pulled up — all seven of them. Roy, who was videotaping the tour, recorded the fire trucks and all the chaos without telling anyone he was the one who had instigated the entire affair at 3 a.m.

The Mayor was a great sport, though. I wasn't sure whether he or Carlton could even swim, but I talked them both into getting certified as divers during the tour. PADI Diving International, one of our major sponsors, had tried in each of the cities we visited to take the crew and get them certified, but we always found we didn't have enough time. At one point, however, we had a swimming pool at the hotel, and we reserved it. I got there early with Roy because he said he didn't know how to swim. I figured if he was going to get certified, he should know how to swim. I was going to teach him. I had him kicking and learning the basics in the shallow end, and he was doing pretty well. He had the dog paddle down and was trying pretty hard. After about half an hour, he was moving fairly well in the shallow end, and I figured we should let him swim a lap, so he jumped in and started his paddling.

Well, what I didn't realize was that he never took a breath of air. He tried to swim from one end to the other, and when he finally got to the deep end he freaked out and started to sink like a rock. I was totally unprepared for this. The guy was sinking to the bottom, and I had to go down and get him. I literally had to drag him off the bottom of the pool and up to the surface. He was dead weight, too, choking and gagging, arms flapping like a fish out of water. I finally pushed him over to the side of the pool and was holding him there while he was spitting and gagging. A couple of my crew members helped me pull him onto the deck. I felt terrible; I had talked him into this ordeal. Here was a guy 50 years old, and I was trying to teach him how to swim in 30 minutes. I felt two inches tall. But Roy didn't seem to mind. After another hour or so, he felt okay. I thought I had scarred him for life as far as swimming is concerned. I didn't think he would ever want to get in the water again. But to my amazement, two walls later, in Key West, Roy did get certified. He's probably the only guy in the world who is a certified diver and doesn't know how to swim.

I have to admire Roy. After I almost killed him, he still came out the next day and helped me finish a wall. What can you say? That's dedication. Roy, for me was one of the most pleasurable parts of the tour. He didn't say much; he just went down and made sure my paint kitchen ran well (I call it my kitchen because that's where I mix up all my special recipes of paint and keep my equipment). He was not only the Mayor, but the chef too. In my opinion, he's a lot better painter than I am, but I'm a better artist, I hope. During a trip with 14 people living closely together almost 24 hours a day for over four months, he never had an unkind word for anybody and got along with the whole crew. He remained even-tempered and always seemed to enjoy the adventure.

The rest of us, however, sometimes would have to rely on external sources to get us through. When times got really tough, we would talk to a little stuffed animal we named "Number Seventeen." It sounds kind of strange, but Number Seventeen got us through when nothing else made any sense. He was a little pink zebra — our little voodoo child. Before I knew it, the number 17 was coming up everywhere I went. I was not just painting 17 murals in 17 cities in 17 weeks, but I had 17 pieces of luggage. I had 17 everything. I was in room 17. . .17 was my life, all summer long — 17, 17, 17.

Besides the Mayor and Number Seventeen, my crew was comprised of some very hard-working, dedicated workers and volunteers. And there are a hundred stories to tell about each one. But I have to say something here about Beavis and Butt-head. Yes, they signed up for this excellent adventure. Only their real names were Daemon and Erik. These guys were classic American "yutes." Daemon was a surfer dude from California, to whom I had promised mega waves if he joined my crew. We didn't see any waves, though. The only waves he saw were at the swimming pool. His board never did get unpacked out of the truck. He still looks at me funny today, but I think he enjoyed the trip anyway. Erik was our cameraman, a good guy except that he probably had the wrong job. Not to knock his work, but I've seen little old ladies with 110 cameras on the freeway get a better pictures of my walls than Erik did. Nonetheless, he was good to have along. He and Daemon were real hard workers.

Another member of the crew was Mike Murray, salesman extraordinaire. Mike has been part of our sales force in Hawaii as well as in California for years. I call him Einstein. He's got wild, gray hair. This guy has hormones that a 16-year-old kid doesn't have. I think he missed his sexual peak when he was young and got it reversed. He's now in his '40s and has the stamina of a teenager. Some of the things that meandered into the art exhibit area were of only Murray's individual desires.

Whale Tales

I knew from the beginning this was going to be a grueling project, but even I underestimated how difficult it would be. By the time we hit Portsmouth, I had to give my Vince Lombardi speech. Mondays and Tuesdays became known as "Muesday," two marathon days that tested the wills and temperaments of the whole crew — I should have provided boxing gloves. They were pretty tired because they had to tear everything down in one city, load up the truck and then unpack and set everything up for the next wall. Most of them had figured out that the exotic ports and women and food and all the things they had been promised was a bunch of bull. This was just going to be a lot of hard work. I sensed that mutiny might be beginning to form so I decided to give my speech and hopefully talk my way out of it. Actually, most of the crew was having a pretty good time. But I thought it was important that I tell them how I felt, and that was that we weren't going to have time to visit the cities as tourists. The reality was that we were the attraction. We were the things the city wanted to see. We were the event, and we should enjoy the journey and enjoy the moment.

It turned out that this was a people tour as well as an art tour. I wanted to make sure we left each city with a signature of our people, who cared and took the time to get to know their city and the people who lived there. We made great and lasting friends at every stop, getting to know the spirit of each of these places and communities. That was priceless. It was a great experience, very rewarding. We were treated in each city as adopted sons, and most times we were given the key to the city. Often, there was a Wyland Day or Wyland Week. And when they said Wyland, I hope they meant Team Wyland. It truly was a team effort, and everybody felt good about it.

The day I was dedicating the Portsmouth wall, I had an urgent call from the Boston Police Department. It seemed they were very concerned with all the media attention the Whaling Wall was generating and that it would cause a major traffic problem on the 93 freeway. The wall site was overlooking this freeway where they estimated a quarter of a million cars would drive past the wall every day. This was the most attractive thing to me, that millions of people a year would see these whales. The idea that the police were ready to cancel the project was very unnerving, and I was hurried to a backroom phone at the mural site to talk to this frantic police officer in charge. I tried to low-key the event, but they knew better. They knew this was going to be major; it was already receiving heavy exposure from all the television and print media throughout Boston. I assured the officer that if traffic did get backed up and people started pulling off the freeway to take pictures of the mural, I would immediately disembark from the scaffolding and wait until traffic cleared. After much prodding, she finally agreed to let the project begin. They informed me that if any problems occurred, they were going to shut it down and, if need be, arrest me on the spot.

The wall had been perfectly primed and was already scaffolded with the swing stage. That morning, I was invited for a dive by *Divers Down*, a television show that features a celebrity diver once a year for a national television program. They wanted me to dive, of all places, in Boston Harbor. They felt that if I could go out there and take a look at the harbor, that maybe I could incorporate some of that history into the mural. I felt it was a good opportunity to get wet, and I always like to get in the water so I agreed. I didn't realize that Boston Harbor was one of the most polluted bodies of water in the United States, and in the world for that matter. In the last five to ten years, though, there have been a lot of groups working to clean it up. *Divers Down* and the local divers were very excited to share that current history of ocean conservation with me.

Now, I don't like cold water. I live in Hawaii for obvious reasons. And when I dive, I like the Caribbean, Mexico or the Great Barrier Reef — warmer climates. I had done some cold water diving, but not for a couple of years. These guys were real hardy, used to diving in much colder water than this, and they assured me the water wasn't that bad. The cameras were ready, and the film crews were set as I, along with six or seven other divers, were escorted down to the water by the Boston Harbor marine police. I climbed into my dry suit with some very thick underwear; everything seemed to be alright. Of course, jumping into Boston Harbor, the visibility was about 10 inches. Everything was green — I couldn't even see my hand in front of my face. It did get a little bit better as we got down to the bottom. I managed to make out some Maine lobsters, and we saw a lot of what looked like new growth — seagrass and other things. It seemed to me the marine life was trying to make a small comeback. We saw various other fish and so on but, to be honest, my teeth were chattering and I was freezing to death. I couldn't wait to get out of there and get back to the wall and start painting.

When we finished the dive, the police boat rushed me back to the dock so I could get to the press conference to announce the Boston Whaling Wall with John Walsh and the World Society for the Protection of Animals. Walsh, a Bostonian and legendary animal rights activist who travels the world saving animals from different disasters, spearheaded this mural. After the press conference, I was anxious to get up there and paint. I didn't want the police to shut the project down. Roy and I got on the scaffolding and immediately started painting masses of color. To my surprise, we covered most of the wall with the background colors, the detail of the ocean's surface and the first lifesize, breaching humpback on the very first day. By the time the sun was setting, the mural looked like it was almost done. People were indeed backing up on the freeway, taking pictures, beeping their horns. Bostonians had the beginnings of their first Whaling Wall and were excited. I'd never seen so many cars nor felt so many eyes looking at me as I was painting. But I seem to enjoy this kind of activity. The crazier it gets the better I paint. I could sense that this was going to be one of my best murals I had ever done.

The next day, Roy and I got on it early and painted another whale below the surface, a female humpback. I also painted something I'd been thinking about for years, a mother humpback pushing her calf to the surface for its first breath. We were beginning to draw some very nice crowds. Some of the volunteers, particularly in Doctor Roger Payne's crew, had brought over some pictures of a humpback that had been seen off of the Massachusetts coastline, a place called Stellwagen Bank. It was a whale everybody knew as Salt. She was called Salt because she had a white, salty patch on her dorsal fin. Humpback whales are unique in that they have tail markings that identify them as individuals. Each one is unique. I had a chance to include Salt's tail markings and her salty white patch on the dorsal fin and portray her individual features. Also, the fact that she was calving there nearly every year was very special in the painting of her portrait. The mural had become not only a lifesize portrait depicting humpback whales, but a picture of an actual whale that had been studied and photographed for over 20 years. That made the project even more special.

Boston had the vision to light the mural. It would be

seen 24 hours a day by over 250,000 cars per day driving by this location. It was going to be one of the most visible murals in the world. We had a special lighting ceremony the night before the dedication. When they flicked the switch for the lights, the mural became three-dimensional. It was like a night dive, hard to describe. We drove on the freeway back and forth several times it was so stunning. As for the police, not a peep. They liked it, too.

The wall in Providence, Rhode Island, went without a hitch and was very helpful to our moral. But New York City was next, and that was a totally different story. We had originally found the perfect wall at the Jacob Javitts Convention Center. It was actually the vent tower for the New York Port Authority Lincoln Tunnel Ventilation Building. After tons of negotiations, we were all ready to sign the paperwork, and Sondra flew to New York with the contract. As luck would have it, the timing couldn't have been worse. The day before, the World Trade Center was bombed by terrorists, and the Port Authority of New York and New Jersey's offices were housed there. Their executives were concerned that if I painted this mural, it would become a target due to all the media covering the New York Whaling

Wall. Scheduled were Bryant Gumbel of NBC's *Today Show*, along with CBS and *Good Morning America*. All three major networks were going to cover us live from New York, which made the Port Authority very nervous. In the 11th hour, they decided there was no way this wall was going to be painted and dedicated on the fourth of July.

I found out later I would've been blown right out of that tower wall on the fourth of July, as the terrorist had planned. But I was determined more than ever to do a wall in New York. When Sondra came back with the news that they had cancelled the New York wall, I gave her one sentence: "Get back on the plane and get me a wall in New York." She looked at me and knew I was serious. She went directly back and persuaded them to find me another location. This was 48 hours before I was to start painting in New York.

We drove from Providence to New York City late at night and pulled up to the Port Authority of New York and New Jersey Bus Terminal on 41st Street, probably one of the most crime ridden, ugly, drug-trafficking, murderous, crack-head, horrible, inner-city locations in New York. It was horrendous. It was like hell down there. I had to literally walk over people living in boxes to get to the wall. It was a scene right out of the apocalypse. As I looked at the wall, I decided that if any environment in the world needed changing, this was it. The great challenge would be to take something so negative and try to make it positive. The wall was part of a dark, black tunnel between the two bus terminals. Over 450 feet long, it was lit with awful, yellow lights. I was hoping the Port Authority, after I was done, would bring some white light down there to showcase the mural as it should be.

I remember seeing the bus terminal in the early '80s on my travels to New York. Then, it was one of the most unsightly and dangerous parts of New York. But now, the inside had been transformed into a much improved, clean center full of vibrant new retail stores and restaurants. It was actually quite nice, but the outside remained very ugly, with garbage and dirt and pollution from the buses and millions of cars. It was grimy — people living in boxes and winos urinating on the wall, my Whaling Wall! You couldn't imagine anything more horrid. Even the cops were afraid to go down there. In fact, all the cops wore bullet proof vests. I was wondering where mine was.

The first day I showed up, a couple of the officers came

over and said, "Hey, how you gonna protect the mural from the winos?"

"Well," I answered, "we've got this anti-graffiti guard clear finish, and it protects against anything."

"Oh yeah?" one of them said. "Come here!" He took me by the arm and walked me across the street. "See that?" He showed me a solid steel door on the side of the alley at the bus depot. The winos had patronized on that door for so many years that the acid content of their urine — thanks to the cheap wine they drank — had melted the steel right off the bottom of the door. "Is your guard gonna protect that?" he asked, a perversely proud smirk planted on his face.

I decided to keep the artwork up high. I would collaborate with the winos regarding the lower part. "We'll call it kelp," I said. "Since this was New York, we could call it modern art."

Once the danger of the bombing had passed, the folks at the Port Authority became very supportive. But I must admit I was nervous painting this wall without a bulletproof vest. The scene going on behind me as I was painting this mural included fist fights between husbands, wives and pimps. People were drinking cheap wine and doing crack in broad daylight. They would ask me if I had a buck, and I would tell them, "I was going to ask you for a buck. I'm an artist." The policy was to dress down to look like we didn't have anything. It wasn't too hard for me because I was covered with paint from head to toe. I was down there in the sewer, between all the buses and noise, pollution and filth. It was a horrible place. I told the Port Authority that since they took care of the inside, I would make sure the outside looked nice. They responded well to that.

We worked on the wall every single day, and it was progressing nicely with some humpback whales. The first night was probably the most memorable because the following morning I was to go on the *Today Show* live at 6 a.m. Jim Fowler, of Mutual of Omaha's *Wild Kingdom* fame, and a friend of mine from years past, was going to come down and interview me. So it was challenging to get the wall to look like something in one day. I raced as fast as I could to cover all the background colors and try to at least get a whale up there. I finished maybe half of the whale the first day. It was probably 2 a.m. and, in that neighborhood, this was quite an experience. The people in the area at that time were not the kind you would want to hang around with. I had most of my crew around me, watching my back.

We finally got back to the hotel, managed a couple of hours sleep and returned at 5 a.m., not only for the *Today Show*, but for *CBS Live*. When I got down there, the network news crews had already been busy. It looked like a major motion picture set, with lights, cameras, makeup crews and my buddy, Jim Fowler. His was the only familiar face in a sea of TV people. He was very warm and pleasant, joined by his wife, Besty, an artist and good friend of mine.

Jim and I were set to air live, and Bryant Gumbel, right out of the shoot, said: "Hey, Wyland, why did you pick this wall in New York? Are there any whales in New York?" I said there were and, fortunately for me, Jim Fowler added: "Yes, Bryant, we had the humpback whales Wyland has depicted right here in the Hudson River." It was great because Jim was helping me out. Then Bryant asked me if we were raising money down there and, if so, what we were doing with it. This was twice he tried to get me.

"Well, Bryant, we're not trying to raise money. . . We're trying to raise the consciousness," I said. After 15 minutes on the *Today Show*, I ran over and did another 15 with CBS. They wanted to get me in there with Roy and get his perspective. It was pretty funny because, during the interview, while the host was talking to Roy, I was standing there with my spray gun and sprayed the heck out of his shirt. The reporter started to laugh hysterically, which, with 40 million people watching, was a great relief. As soon as they left, we got back to work and completed the mural in only five days. I dedicated this mural to Jim Fowler, whom I had enjoyed for many years on television when I was growing up. He came back and signed the wall with me during a special ceremony on July 5th.

We were really looking forward to the next wall in the old whaling village of New London, Connecticut. What we weren't looking forward to, however, was the intense heat wave that had just moved in. It had already killed over 100 people, and the heat generated off the wall was right in my face. Angela had a heat stroke. Roy caught her just before she hit the pavement. A couple of hours later, I suffered a heat stroke, too, for the first time in my life. My legs wobbled and caved in, and I had to be taken where there was some air conditioning and wet rags to recover.

After New London, we painted a very high wall in Philadelphia that had exceptional visibility from all parts of downtown, including the Amtrack Station. We then did a mural in Wildwood, New Jersey, which, ecstatic over beating out Atlantic City for the project, was the most enthusiastic of all the cities on the tour. Literally hundreds of thousands of people came down to see the wall, including thousands of kids I could talk to and teach about the whales. The Harley-Davidson Riders of New Jersey also came down and made me one of their "bros" by giving me a jacket and loaning me a Harley to ride.

From Wildwood, we traveled to Wilmington, Delaware, where I painted a diptych showing only above-water scenes. And we moved on to Washington, D.C., where I painted a mural at the National Zoo. Even though this was the smallest wall on the tour, we called it the "Mighty Wall" because it was right at the entrance to the zoo — five million people would walk right by it every year. I felt if I was going to paint the smallest Whaling Wall, I would need to paint the smallest whales, the dolphins, which are actually small-tooth whales. Dr. Roger Payne, to whom I dedicated this mural, suggested I paint a harbor porpoise, which is the smallest of the dolphins. I thought it was an incredible idea and painted the harbor porpoise in his honor. He was gracious enough to fly in from London to dedicate the mural at a very special ceremony. Afterward, we discussed a possible special on my work for Discovery Television. The dedication was attended by many of Washington's political circles, and the World Wildlife Fund and the National Wildlife Federation gave their accolades. We also had a front-page story in *The Washington Post*, which was a nice surprise.

I had been wanting to do a mural on the National Aquarium in Baltimore for a long time. But, when we got there, we came across the aquarium director, Nick Brown, who in my opinion, had no vision whatsoever. Since having the mural painted on the aquarium was not his idea, it did not have his blessing or approval. He tried to sabotage the project every way he could. What was ironic was that I had just finished a wall at the National Zoo, and here was the National Aquarium — the most appropriate place to have a Whaling Wall — and its director was trying to stop the mural for his own selfish purposes. He had influenced a lot of city officials and the architect, and together they opposed the project. My supporters, however, agreed that it was important to continue to try and gain approval for the mural. At one point, I said I would paint two murals in Baltimore.

We were running out of time so we started with the wall across the street from Camden Yards. This site was very attractive and would actually see more traffic on the main road than the National Aquarium. But I still thought the National Aquarium was the most appropriate.

My argument was that a blank wall does nothing to stimulate people, whereas a Whaling Wall would present the great whales on a grand scale and make an impact as only the whales themselves could. With all the controversy over animals in captivity and animals in aquariums, this was a tremendous opportunity for the National Aquarium to feature great whales, lifesize, through public art and education, and save face. Everything about it was perfect. The problem I had was with the architect and the director. It seemed like the only things they wanted to save were their egos. I was willing to take these two knuckleheads on but, when we eventually dedicated the Baltimore mural, Nick Brown, the director, resigned the same day. So, thank you City of Baltimore. Thank you everybody who saw fit to bug the holy hell out of this guy with faxes, letters and phone calls. Mahalo!

As for the architect, Peter Chermayeff, he was driving on the freeway past the Boston Whaling Wall when, over his car phone, he told a reporter: "This Boston wall is fantastic, but not in my neighborhood, not on my aquarium, not on my architecture. That is a work of art itself. Why would we want a mural?" The Sistine Chapel was a work of art, too, but is better known for the work of Michelangelo, not the architect.

What the hell? The Baltimore mural was complete. For the first time, I had painted an extinct species of whales, the Atlantic gray whales, which were wiped out in the early 17th century by American Yankee whalers. I wanted to bring attention to this with an extinction mural. It raised a lot of questions. Anytime you can tell a story and get your message across, then you're doing what you're supposed to do with your art.

In Norfolk, Virginia, I was battling the flu and seriously wondering if I could finish their wall, which was over 400 feet long and eight stories high. The tour was starting to take its toll. Somehow, though, Roy and I worked all day, every day, and the mural turned out to be one of my best. Tens of thousands of people came down to watch, and it was fun to watch from our sixth-story perch the police putting up yellow tape to control the crowd. Then they took that down and put up some wooden barriers. Eventually, they closed down the whole street. Afterward, we dedicated the wall to Jacques Cousteau. Angela and I had the rare opportunity to visit The Cousteau Society in nearby Chesapeake, Virginia, and meet some of his dedicated staff. I left one of my bronze sculptures for Mr. Cousteau, who was away in Europe at the time. He later wrote me a very nice letter thanking me for the piece.

We quickly finished a small wall in Wilmington, North Carolina. We had chosen a larger wall earlier, but the mayor caved in to some local idiots, and we ended up painting a postage stamp mural instead of a real Whaling Wall. But it turned out really nice, and thousands of people made the pilgrimage to Wilmington to watch me paint it.

Then we drove to Myrtle Beach, our 14th mural in 14 weeks. We were exhausted, but we could see the light at the end of the tunnel. The people there were very warm, just like the city. School was coming into session, and the city made the Whaling Wall their number-one priority so they could start busing these kids in for this public art event. Whenever I saw a group down there, I would go down and spend some time with them. At one point, about 600 kids came to meet me... Wow! What was great about them was that they knew more about marine art than I ever did at their age. And about saving the ocean. Some of them, by the way, are better artists than I was. And that's always encouraging to me. I love to see it. They are so excited and honest about everything. We figured that by the end of the tour, I had talked to over 70,000 children. That's another great thing that came out of the tour. One kid asked when I was going to stop talking and start painting.

I painted right whales at Myrtle Beach, the first time I had done it in the States. It was appropriate because they had right whales off the coast. Also, I knew I would be painting right whales for Atlanta, and I knew that was going to be the biggest mural on the tour. I wanted to be sure I could still paint them. The last right whales I had painted were in Taiji, Japan. The Myrtle Beach mural really was quite easy and seemed to paint itself. With all the support of the community, it was a good time.

Everyone was excited when we reached Atlanta. This was our 50th Whaling Wall, the half-way mark in my goal of painting 100 around the world. It also is where the Olympics will be held and is a huge wall, 450 feet long and over seven stories high. It would be one of the largest murals in the Eastern United States. It fronted the Coca-Cola Museum and had tremendous visibility from all parts of the city. We had a crazy pilot from Delta Airlines named Dave Mattingly coordinating the project. Dave was a wild, woman-loving guy who managed to get all of these beautiful flight attendants as volunteers. I'm not complaining. It was a lot of fun and, being that it was the 50th Whaling Wall, it was very special to me. Besides, I only look at whales. . . right?

This wall had been there for 30 years, and every artist and every advertiser wanted to paint on it. But nobody could get permission. Our friend Dave, however, wasn't to be denied. He just stayed on it until they said yes. I'm so glad he did because this mural is in the best location in Atlanta. Hopefully, with the Olympics coming, it will be one of the best landmarks in the city.

In Sarasota, the Mote Marine Laboratory had wanted me to do a Whaling Wall for several years. Mike Martin, who is a good friend and happens to be on the board of directors over there, coordinated everything. I felt it was very important to do a mural for this new marine mammal facility they had built to help stranded marine mammals. When I was about to finish this mural, I invited Mike to come up on the scaffolding since he had spearheaded the project. We weren't up there 10 minutes, and all we had to do was paint a few fish and the mural would be complete. Mike suddenly turned to hand me a brush when he accidentally kicked a can of black paint and it went all over the whole mural. His face turned white. He was frantic, but I was laughing. I just said it looked like seagrass to me. It covered the entire bottom half of the wall with black. He was hysterical. I got down and tried to hose it off, but it was too late. So I incorporated it into the seagrass and named him as an assistant painter. Even though he was embarrassed over it, I thought it was funny, and we razed him unmercifully.

There was an "art critic" working for *The Sarasota Herald-Tribune* named Joan Altabe. This lady must have had a split personality. The first story she did on me, she called me the "master of the concrete canvas." The next story, she attacked me, calling me a graffiti artist and a nobody. The next one was incredible, a tremendous story, followed by another attack. She didn't know which way she was going. It was funny because she was supposedly the big art critic in town, and she attacked *all* the artists. A friend of mine, Jack

Dowd, a great woodcarver respected around the world as a fine artist and sculptor, made a t-shirt with her face on it and a red cross across her face — "Just Say No to Joan." After her last article defaming me and telling me to get out of town, people were outraged. At the dedication, the mayor, on top of giving me the key to the city, handed me a proclamation saying I was an honorary citizen. I remember saying: "Now that I'm an honorary citizen, I think I'll stay and Joan Altabe should get out of town." The mayor smiled and everyone gave me and the crew a standing ovation. Jack Dowd then presented me with the t-shirt, and we held it up in victory. I think it was the first time an art critic got it right back in her face. She hasn't been seen or heard from since. Maybe they rode her out of town on a rail. This lady was unusually nasty. The Ringling School of Art, one of the top-rated art schools in the nation, came to my rescue saying how nice it was for me to lecture and talk to their students and let them volunteer to help out on the mural. To quote the great Bart Simpson: "Up hers!"

On the entire East Coast Tour, we only ran into two jerks, both frustrated artists who had become art critics and were failures at both.

Whale Tales

We finally made it down to Key West, one of my favorite towns in Florida and in all of the United States. I love the Keys for diving and have spent a lot of my years down there looking at America's only living reef on the Mainland. I spent some of my best vacations in high school and college down there. I had already painted a wall in the Marathon Keys a few years earlier, but Key West was where it was at. We were working with a very well known group called Reef Relief, which had done some great work to design buoys to protect the reef, and replace the anchors that would damage it. They were also involved in a lot of clean water efforts and were to spearhead the Whaling Wall project. Unfortunately, the wall I wanted to paint on the Waterfront Playhouse, where the sunset festivities are held each evening, was shot down by a small group of people. Reef Relief found another location that was actually larger, and they felt it would become a major landmark after the mural was completed. My crew and I were relieved just to be in Key West, knowing this was the last mural on the tour and we would get a well deserved rest. I told everyone they could have a week off, on me, and they were sure ready for it after a long extremely hot summer. We were upbeat and excited to be there. We all went out and rented mopeds and became moped bikers. Key West was very supportive, and there were a lot of crazy characters there. At last, this was the final wall.

What I had envisioned immediately after looking at the wall was Florida's living reef. I had been thinking about it for years. The wall was not very large, but in a good location. It had a huge impact and became a local favorite as soon as we started painting.

Another great thing about the Keys was that we had decided that everyone on the crew was going to finally get certified as divers, even Roy, no matter what. To my surprise, Roy actually did. Everyone did. While they were all out diving, I was finishing the mural. I wanted to dive, too, but my priority was to finish this last wall and make it the best it could be, which is not to say we didn't partake in what Key West had to offer. In fact, we partied very hard and celebrated almost every night. The night I remembered most was the evening we had a roast. The crew had a private dinner, which our crew called our "Last Supper," and everybody got to get up there to give a gift and tell a story about another person on the crew. It was very, very funny. I can't go into detail, but Daemon, after he told his story, looked me straight in the eye and said, "Bite me." He had had enough. We were at the end of our journey, and the admiration I felt for each member of the crew I can't begin to put into words. They were just unselfishly great.

Key West was fantastic. Captain Tony, the former mayor and co-owner of Captain Tony's, and a good friend of Jimmy Buffet's, came down and dedicated the wall with the current mayor. It was dedicated to the people of Key West and to Reef Relief and their efforts. Spirits were very high. We were ready to enjoy Key West and then get back home. After four months of working sunup to sundown, living in hotel rooms and being in the public eye, I was ready to go down to the Caribbean. We were heading for St. Lucia to enjoy some quality time underwater.

Back home on the beautiful North Shore of Oahu, thinking of all the good times we had and the bad, and everything we went through, was a tremendous feeling. It was a hell of a time, and we accomplished the impossible. This was the miracle tour, and we actually made it look easy.

When's the next one? Would you like to go? There'll be exotic ports. . . beautiful women. . . wonderful food. . . big bucks. . . time off. . . . . .

With Warm Aloha!

WYLAND

Whale Tales

Wyland Galleries
L o c a t i o n s

LAGUNA BEACH
2171 Laguna Canyon Rd
Laguna Beach, CA 92651
(800) 777-0039•(714) 497-4081

OAHU
94-130 Leokane Street
Waipahu, HI 96797-2209
(800) 992-7498•(808) 676-7498

LAGUNA BEACH
218 Forest Avenue
Laguna Beach, CA 92651
(714) 497-9494

OAHU
66-150 Kamehameha Hwy
Haleiwa, HI 96712
(800) 578-6248•(808) 637-7498

SAN DIEGO
855 W. Harbor Drive
San Diego, CA 92101
(619) 544-9995

OAHU
2424 Kalakaua
Honolulu, HI 96815
(808) 924-3133

LONG BEACH
4814 E. 2nd Street
Lonag Beach, CA 90803
(310) 987-3830

HONOLULU
2155 Kalakaua Ave #104
Honolulu, HI 96815
(808) 924-1322

PORTLAND
711 SW 10th Avenue
Portland, OR 97205
(800) 578-7316•(503) 223-7692

MAUI
136 Dickenson Street
Lahaina, HI 96761
(800) 578-6284•(808) 661-0690

KEY WEST
717 Duval Street
Key West, FL 33040
(305) 292-9711

MAUI
2435 Kaanapali Parkway
Lahaina, HI 96761
(808) 661-8255

HAWAII
Waikoloa Beach Resort
Waikoloa, HI 96743
(808) 578-5258

MAUI
711 Front Street
Lahaina, HI 96761
(808) 667-2285

HAWAII
75-5770 Alli Drive
Kailua-Kona, HI 96740
(808) 334-0037

MAUI
697 Front Street
Lahaina, HI 96761
(808) 661-7099

HAWAII
Waikoloa Beach Resort
Waikoloa, HI 96738
(808) 885-8882

KAUI
2360 Kiahuna Plantation Dr
Koloa, HI 96756
(808) 742-6030

KAUAI
3416 Rice Street
Lihue, HI 96766
(808) 246-0702

WHALING WALL LOCATIONS

1981 WHALING WALL 1 - "GREY WHALE AND CALF"
LAGUNA BEACH, CALIFORNIA
140 FEET LONG X 26 FEET HIGH

1982 WHALING WALL 2 - "YOUNG GREY WHALE"
DANA POINT, CALIFORNIA
45 FEET LONG X 10 FEET HIGH

1984 WHALING WALL 3 - "SPYHOPPING"
RANCHO PALOS VERDES, CA.
20 FEET LONG X 30 FEET HIGH

1984 WHALING WALL 4
"THE GREY WHALE FAMILY"
WHITEROCK, BRITISH COLUMBIA, CANADA
70 FEET LONG X 30 FEET HIGH

1985 WHALING WALL 5
"THE ORCAS OF PUGET SOUND"
SEATTLE, WASHINGTON
140 FEET LONG X 50 FEET HIGH

1985 WHALING WALL 6 - "HAWAIIAN HUMPBACKS"
HONOLULU, HAWAII
300 FEET LONG X 20 STORIES HIGH (1/2 ACRE)

1985 WHALING WALL 7
"CALIFORNIA GREY WHALES"
DEL MAR, CA.
100 FEET LONG X 16 FEET HIGH

1985 WHALING WALL 8 - "ORCAS"
VANCOUVER, BRITHISH COLUMBIA, CANADA
130 FEET LONG X 70 FEET HIGH

1986 WHALING WALL 9 - "FIRST VOYAGE"
OAHU, HI
130 FEET LONG X 14 FEET HIGH

1986 WHALING WALL 10 - "MANATEES"
ORLANDO, FLORIDA
14 FEET LONG X 8 FEET HIGH

1986 WHALING WALL 11 - "FIRST BORN"
SEA WORLD, ORLANDO, FLORIDA
30 FEET LONG X 12 FEET HIGH

1987 WHALING WALL 12 - "LAGUNA COAST"
2171 LAGUNA CANYON RD.
LAGUNA BEACH, CALIF
20 FEET LONG X 24 FEET HIGH

1987 WHALING WALL 13 - "A-5 POD"
VICTORIA, BRITISH COLUMBIA, CANADA
130 FEET LONG X 7 STORIES HIGH

1987 WHALING WALL 14 - "SPERM WHALES"
FUNABASHI, JAPAN
140 FEET LONG X 18 FEET HIGH

1988 WHALING WALL 15
"DOLPHINS OFF MAKAPUU POINT"
SEA LIFE PARK, OAHU, HAWAII
24 FEET LONG X 30 FEET HIGH

1989 WHALING WALL 16 - "ORCAS OFF POINT LOMA"
THE PLUNGE MISSION BEACH
SAN DIEGO, CA
140 FEET LONG X 40 FEET HIGH

1989 WHALING WALL 17 - "BOTTLENOSE DOLPHINS"
OSAKA, JAPAN
20 FEET LONG X 30 FEET HIGH

1989 WHALING WALL 18
"SPERM WHALES OF THE MEDITERRANEAN"
NICE, FRANCE
42 FEET LONG X 120 FEET HIGH

1989 WHALING WALL 19 - "FORBIDDEN REEF"
SEA WORLD, SAN DIEGO, CA
90 FEET LONG X 14 FEET HIGH

1990 WHALING WALL 20
"GREY WHALE MIGRATION"
SEA WORLD, SAN DIEGO, CA
80 FEET LONG X 15 FEET HIGH

1990 WHALING WALL 21 - "WASHINGTON ORCAS"
TACOMA, WASHINGTON
120 FEET LONG X 45 FEET HIGH

1990 WHALING WALL 22 (CEILING)
"ORCA HEAVEN"
YAMAGATA, JAPAN
145 FEET LONG X 45 FEET HIGH

1990 WHALING WALL 23
"BUNDABERG HUMPBACK FAMILY"
BUNDABERG, AUSTRALIA
125 FEET LONG X 95 FEET HIGH

1990 WHALING WALL 24
"HUMPBACK AND CALF"
SYDNEY AQUARIUM, SYDNEY, AUSTRALIA
90 FEET LONG X 35 FEET HIGH

1990 WHALING WALL 25 - "HUMPBACKS"
LAMPHERE HIGH SCHOOL, DETROIT, MI.
110 FEET LONG X 15 FEET HIGH

1990 WHALING WALL 26
"SPERM WHALES AND FLORIDA KEYES REEF"
MARATHON KEYES, FLORIDA
150 FEET LONG X 20 FEET HIGH

1990 WHALING WALL 27 - "MINKI WHALES"
MARATHON KEYES, FLORIDA
40 FEET LONG X 8 FEET HIGH

1991 WHALING WALL 28
"A TIME FOR CONSERVATION"
KAUAI VILLAGE, KAUAI, HAWAII
44 FEET HIGH WALL, 360 DEGREE MURAL

1991 WHALING WALL 29
"ALOHA SPIRIT"
KAUAI , HAWAII
150 FEET LONG X 24 FEET HIGH

WHALING WALL LOCATIONS

1991 WHALING WALL 30
"MAUI HUMPBACK BREACHING"
LAHAINA, MAUI, HAWAII
26 FEET LONG X 30 FEET HIGH

1991 WHALING WALL 31
"GREY WHALE MIGRATION"
REDONDO BEACH, CALIFORNIA
586 FEET LONG X 100 FEET HIGH (1 1/4 ACRE)

1991 WHALING WALL 32 - "WHALES"
TAIJI, JAPAN
30 FEET X 60 FEET

1992 WHALING WALL 33 - "PLANET OCEAN"
LONG BEACH, CALIFORNIA
1,280 FEET LONG X 105 FEET HIGH
GUINNESS WORLD BOOK OF RECORDS
MAY 4, 1992

1993 WHALING WALL 34
"OCEAN BIOSPHERE" BIOSPHERE 2
ORACLE, ARIZONA
110 FEET LONG X 30 FEET HIGH

1993 WHALING WALL 35
"ORCAS OF THE OREGON COAST"
PORTLAND, OREGON
120 FEET LONG X 60 FEET HIGH

1993 WHALING WALL 36
"WHALES OFF THE GULF OF MAINE"
PORTLAND, MAINE
1,000 FEET LONG X 25 FEET HIGH

1993 WHALING WALL 37
"ISLE OF SHOALS HUMPBACKS"
PORTSMOUTH, NEW HAMPSHIRE
220 FEET LONG X 40 FEET HIGH

1993 WHALING WALL 38
"STELLWAGEN BANK HUMPBACKS"
BOSTON, MASSACHUSETTS
110 FEET LONG X 125 FEET HIGH

1993 WHALING WALL 39
"FINACK WHALES"
PROVIDENCE, RHODE ISLAND
280 FEET LONG X 24 FEET HIGH

1993 WHALING WALL 40
"INNER CITY WHALES"
NEW YORK, NEW YORK
460 FEET LONG X 22 FEET HIGH

1993 WHALING WALL 41
"THE GREAT SPERM WHALES"
NEW LONDON, CONNECTICUT
170 FEET LONG X 35 FEET HIGH

1993 WHALING WALL 42
"EAST COAST HUMPBACKS"
PHILADELPHIA, PENNSYLVANIA
125 FEET LONG X 130 FEET HIGH

1993 WHALING WALL 43
"HUMPBACKS OFF THE JERSEY COAST"
WILDWOOD, NEW JERSEY
220 FEET LONG X 30 FEET HIGH

1993 WHALING WALL 44
"DELAWARE MARINE MAMMALS"
WILMINGTON, DELAWARE
90 FEET LONG X 60 FEET HIGH

1993 WHALING WALL 45
"DOLPHINS - SMALL TOOTH WHALES"
WASHINGTON, D.C.
30 FEET LONG X 15 FEET HIGH

1993 WHALING WALL 46
"EXTINCT ATLANTIC GRAY WHALES"
BALTIMORE, MARYLAND
260 FEET LONG X 20 FEET HIGH

1993 WHALING WALL 47
"HUMPBACKS OFF VIRGINA COAST"
NORFOLK, VIRGINIA
22,400 SQ. FT. - 280 FEET LONG X 80 FEET HIGH

1993 WHALING WALL 48
"COASTAL DOLPHINS"
WILMINGTON, NORTH CAROLINA
40 FEET LONG X 30 FEET HIGH

1993 WHALING WALL 49
"RIGHT WHALES OFF THE S. CAROLINA COAST"
MYRTLE BEACH, SOUTH CAROLINA
250 FEET LONG X 50 FEET HIGH

1993 WHALING WALL 50
"ATLANTA'S RIGHTWHALES"
ATLANTA, GEORGIA
450 FEET LONG X 5 STORIES (50 FEET) HIGH

1993 WHALING WALL 51
"FLORIDA'S DOLPHINS"
SARASOTA, FLORIDA
45' LONG X 26 ' HIGH

1993 WHALING WALL 52
"FLORIDA'S LIVING REEF"
KEY WEST, FLORIDA
52 FEET LONG X 45 FEET HIGH

1994 WHALING WALL 53
"ORCAS OFF THE GULF OF MEXICO"
SOUTH PADRE ISLAND, TEXAS
265 FEET X 25 FEET HIGH

1994 **WEST COAST WHALING WALL TOUR:**
ANCHORAGE, ALASKA - AUGUST
VANCOUVER, BRITISH COLUMBIA - AUGUST
SEATTLE, WASHINGTON - AUGUST
NEWPORT, OREGON - AUGUST
SAN FRANCISCO, CALIFORNIA - AUGUST
LOS ANGELES, CALIFORNIA - SEPTEMBER
SAN DIEGO, CALIFORNIA - SEPTEMBER
MEXICO CITY, MEXICO - SEPTEMBER

Whale Tales